Further Praise for
THE FIFTH CHAMBER

"A piercing, devastating, and tender text, this book sees what it means
be broken and built back up again, by grief and by love, but yes, most
all, by love."

—Janice Lee, author of *Imagine a Death and Separation Anxiety*

"I gulped this book. I wept this book . . . Read this book, for the hun-
, tender heart you have, for the heart you long to remember."

—Jen Violi, author of *Putting Makeup on Dead People*

"There's no one, and I mean no one, who writes like Anne Gudger. A
m to the heart and a hug and an 'It's so good, I wish I wrote that' kind
beautiful."

—Jennifer Pastiloff, bestselling author of *On Being Human*

THE FIFTH CHAMBER

A MEMOIR

BY ANNE GUDGER

Cover and interior book design: Nicole Roberts
Cover art illutrator: Karen Luke Fildes
Bookends illustrator: Katie Guinn
Author photo: Robin Damore

This book is also available in electronic book format.

Gudger, Anne

The Fifth Chamber / Gudger

Dedicated to Kent, my first husband, who died too soon, whom I searched for in all the places. And to Scot, my thirty-three year and more husband, whom I found in all the places. To my phenomenal son and daughter, Jacob and Maria, who've held my heart since before they drew breath: this is for you.

I give you my work of memory—of impressions. What stayed from then. What stays now. I wrote these pages as memory allows, with some name changes—especially those across years and miles.

If You Knew

What if you knew you'd be the last
to touch someone?
If you were taking tickets, for example,
at the theater, tearing them,
giving back the ragged stubs,
you might take care to touch that palm,
brush your fingertips
along the life line's crease.

When a man pulls his wheeled suitcase
too slowly through the airport, when
the car in front of me doesn't signal,
when the clerk at the pharmacy
won't say *Thank you,* I don't remember
they're going to die.

A friend told me she'd been with her aunt.
They'd just had lunch and the waiter,
a young gay man with plum black eyes,
joked as he served the coffee, kissed
her aunt's powdered cheek when they left.
Then they walked half a block and her aunt
dropped dead on the sidewalk.

How close does the dragon's spume
have to come? How wide does the crack
in heaven have to split?
What would people look like
if we could see them as they are,
soaked in honey, stung and swollen,
reckless, pinned against time?

—Ellen Bass

RTS. ELASTIC....
HARD WORKING
POUNDED · STRETCHED · FIST-SHAPED MUSCLE
SLIPPERY TIME KEEPER
LOVE YOU WITH ALL
Te amo co
TRIUM
BOOM BOOM
BOOM BOOM
SWISH
FIFTH CHAMBER
Right Ventricle
ART HOLE STITCHED with Lightning
PEPPER SLIMI
LEFT
NTRICLE

THE FIFTH CHAMBER

Prologue

I thought I was broken, and for a while I was. In the belly of my grief, I couldn't see any gold, not a fleck—no gold leaf wrinkle, no first star in a night sky, no purple-gold shimmer of oil in a puddle, no hint of the kintsugi of me. Kintsugi: the Japanese art of honoring the broken—filling cracks with gold, elevating the beauty of what was, seeing it as greater because of its fissures and splits, because of its story. Before the gold there must be the break.

Before the break there's a different wholeness.

After

Nestled on the bottom of the ocean. Lightless. Black past zero—the blackest black. Me in a half lotus. Half because my lunar baby belly disappeared my lap and shrank my legs. Half lotus me with fisheyes that stared sideways. Fish gills I was sure would fail if I dared to swim to the surface. A hole in my heart where love leaked into the sea.

You're going to be okay, people said, like this was true. Didn't they know nothing would ever be okay again?

You're going to be okay sounded like: You-rrrrre-go-ingggg-to-beeee-o-kaaaa, in my underwater world. In the cold of deep water. In the ice of me.

I flicked my dead husband's boy ID bracelet against my wrist. This kid-sized steel bracelet with his name engraved in four letters: *Kent.* The stretchy metal band dug in. Tiny crisscross marks etched a wrist map.

My mermaid sister swam down to the bottom of the sea. She wrapped me in her arms. She wrapped me in her muscle mermaid tale. She wrapped me in love.

Swim with me to the surface, she said, and I stared at the bubbles bubbling from her perfect *O* mermaid mouth, her ruby lips. I cried tsunami tears in her hair. I shook my head. No.

It's your fish baby's time, she said, her words extra on *your* and *time*.

There's a trail of memories, like stepping stones, we can follow to the above, she said, flicking her mermaid shimmer tail. Even in the black I could see her scales, rows of metallic blue-emerald sequins stitched in waves up and down and around her mermaid body.

I dug my chin into my chest, her chest, my hair, her hair.

What if your fish boy wants to see the moon in the night sky? she asked.

I'm right here, she said and cradled my hand in the wet of hers. We'll learn to breathe air together.

When my boy was born in a frigid hospital room with celadon walls, harsh lights, steel trays, Pine-Sol colliding with blood smells.

When the umbilical cord was wrapped around his neck. Twice. Blue Boy. Blueberry crossed with baby blue. Limp baby. Puddle baby. No wiggle. No flex. No air trapped in his tiny lungs. All the air trapped in mine.

When Dr. H unfurled that slimy cord with sausage fingers. Unfurled. Once. Twice. And my fish boy who swam to me who swam through me who swam out of me, gasped and cried. Fish boy cry flooded the cool room.

When he wobbled his head and looked through me with his sea-blue eyes. Not sky blue like his dead dad's. Deep water blue.

Check him for scales, I asked/told my mermaid sister, ocean water dripping from the ends of her hair, pooling at her toes.

My cleaved heart throbbed. Thundered. Whispered.

Count fingers and toes, I asked/told my mom who only repeated in a loop: You have a boy. A beautiful boy.

This boy. Hair dark as a wet log. Honey skin. Lungs with their web of bronchi like naked winter trees. Lungs with cry power. Pierce the dark power. My fish boy: six pounds, nine ounces of yum.

A love tsunami flooded the hole in my heart, stitched it with filaments of blue bliss, stitched it with gossamer threads from the ocean, from the night sky.

This pink boy on my chest.

Skin to skin.

Forehead to forehead.

Love tent.

My cells in him.

His cells in me.

Hummingbird heart to whale heart.

A tiny seed, a spore of goodness, micro as an orchid seed—the smallest seed in the flower world—burrowed into my heart muscle, carved a pocket where atria and ventricles meet. This fifth chamber tendrilled roots, rooted a pinprick of hope in my heart that I thought was broken.

He strained his wobbly head to my voice. Eyes of ocean and sky and the in-between place where sky bumps sea. I saw past day and dark, past rivers of light, past celestial bodies. Through the worm of time. Backwards and forwards. I had flashes of me at 5 twirling in a stick-out slip like a tutu, at 9 riding my horse Gina, at 13 sketching, at 16 learning to drive a Fiat stick-shift, at 18 leaving for college, graduating, then marrying Kent on a steamy August day by a lake with our families circled around and a trumpeting swan too, then Europe and ocean and backpacking, skiing with my growing belly, Kent skiing without me, the chaplain in the dark of night, the chaplain with his grey eyes, grey words. To here. This moment. My boy's birth. I flashed ahead—snapshots of him in his Batman cape, playing with Spiderman, building Legos, chasing our dog, dragging sticks, poking dirt and rocks, splashing in puddles. Grinning. Laughing his boy laugh that would crack the world.

I love you, Baby, I whispered, since I didn't know his name. I didn't know much but I did know that.

I kissed his soft spot—that tender diamond-shaped spot on his crown, his fontanelle where the frontal and parietal bones hadn't fused. Fontanelle, like *fountain*, *fondness*, maybe *faith* and *fairies* too, where the skull is vulnerable, where I smelled the cosmos.

This perfect tiny human. He grew from tangles of love chromosomes, dark matter, starlight, star atoms, oceans of hearts. Grew from love and lust and legacy and want. Split into boy. Picked long and slender from the gene pool—piano player fingers and elegant feet (Just like Kent's! my mermaid sister said.) Mini finger/toenails like the insides of seashells, pink and shiny.

I circled his chest with two hands, my thumbtips and middle fingertips stretching to touch. *Someday you'll be a man*, I thought. *And I'll show you your tininess when you first arrived.* This *O* of thumbs to fingers. This *O* of astonishment. This *O* of a love profound.

And my heart I thought was pulp, beat strong. Muscle heart. Slimy. Pink. Not black. Not shrunken. Bigger than my fist. Swollen with love. Bass drum drumming. Once beaten. Still beating.

I was always here, it whispered. I never gave up on you.

Could I be broken *and* happy?

The heart of it all.

Boom, boom, swish. Thrumming heart. Tough and tender. Caged and untamable. Small as a Comice pear. Big as sky. Milky Way heart. Oceanic heart.

After

I got it, I voiced in a loop when I had to do all the hard things. My mantra to myself, family, friends, co-teachers, my neighbor John, the diaper delivery driver I startled a few times before 5:00 a.m. I got it. Except when I didn't. No glossing up my not-got-it-ness, my overcooked rawness.

My husband died when I was six months pregnant, and I thought I lost everything. Then, I didn't have it. Then, I cried tsunamis and burrowed in bed through endless days cradling my beat-up heart, begging the world to halt, to freeze with me. Three months after Kent died, after Jake was born, even though I was pulp, I whispered I got it when I slumped from my sloshing waterbed while my body craved the numb of sleep. I got it. Because babies need boobs and dry diapers. Because squashed as I was, I'd never give up on my boy.

Sometimes I'd half-roll to the cool side of the bed and say: My turn. I'll get him this time. When Jake woke at 2:08 a.m., 4:13 a.m. when the digital numbers glowed to my left and streetlight crept in through the mini blinds on my right. In that in-between time. Not morning. Not night.

Somehow saying my turn—even though every turn was mine—helped me feel like Kent was with me, like maybe he'd claim the next shift.

I didn't believe *I got it* when my spine crumbled to a bone pile. Me, face down, sobbing on the stairs, not remembering if I was going up or down. I didn't believe it when I cried hard and fast, no warm-up, no pinched nose or thick between my ears, when the Safeway checker asked, Lady, are you okay? as I stared at my new checks with only my name in the upper left corner. Or when I blanked out in the middle of scratching words on the chalkboard (Quote? Assignment?) while teaching English 101. When a colleague held newborn Jake and cooed at him: It's so sad you don't have a dad. When my inner compass spun. All that and more landed in the Fuck It pile.

Fuck it to the days and moons I wasn't sure about anything.

I got it helped me breathe and make puny moves.

Outranked by Fuck It.

Before

The swoosh and glide of backcountry skis, as we carved our way deeper into the woods. Kent and I bobbed a little forward and backward, a little side to side under the weight of our packs. Winter followed us everywhere. Evergreen branches sagged with snow, with the weight of all those snowflakes clumped together. Northwest blue sky pierced the trees. Winter sun doused everything in leggy shadows.

Kent cut the trail, all army green backpack with legs. At almost twice my weight, he carried more than I did, including the extra water, most of the food and cookware, plus a 20-pound climbing rope. Thank the backpacking stars. The summer before, when I spent 30 days on a mountaineering course in Wyoming, all 15 students carried about the same weight: 60 pounds. There was no recalibrating weight based on size. At five-foot-two I packed as much as the six-foot-tall guys. One of the many How to Be a Good Mountaineer rules of the National Outdoor Leadership School: Carry your own weight.

What? Kent said when I told him I packed 60 pounds, hiked about 10 miles a day—eight to ten hours—with my beasty pack pressing me down, knocking me over until I learned to wrangle it.

You all carried the same weight? he asked with a head shake. That's kinda nuts. Are you okay with me carrying more when we go?

Please do!

I'll always be proud I carried that monster pack. I needed to show myself I could, and I did. I grinned huge at the memory. How I dug deep that month. How I wouldn't let blisters or bruises or exhaustion or harsh words stop me. How every cut and bug bite and ego-slamming moment became a badge of I Did It seared into my heart.

On a flat stretch, Kent slowed and stopped. He leaned on his ski poles, turned and beamed at me. The dimple and cleft chin of him. The swimming pool blue eyes of him.

You okay, Annie? Breath clouds bubbled around his words.

I'm great! I half-shouted. My galloping heart pressed against my chest strap. This hard-working heart that beat extra in the push and glide of skiing, that beat extra in bliss: with this honey of a man I was mush for, surrounded by Mama Nature, decked out in glitter snow that winked in the sun. No car tracks. No shoveled paths. A sea of white against a sky as blue as my love's eyes.

How about we camp here?

I skated up to Kent, all six feet, two hundred pounds of him. Steely grey hair. Coyote-colored beard with streaks of cinnamon. Grin cradled between freckled cheeks.

My sister's friends called me Howdy Doody when I was little, he had said one time, and I had to admit I could see it: his round face and freckles and crooked teeth. This man carved from

Colorado mountains, tempered by Caltech's physics department, married, almost divorced. I struggled with the almost divorced.

I promise the divorce is happening, he had said on our first date, our downhill skiing date when I asked buckets of questions, when he told me Yes, he was married and not really married, when my palms cooled inside my gloves and I inched away from him on the chairlift chugging us up the mountainside.

How close are you to being divorced? I asked. It's okay if you're not close, I started, telling myself not to bite my lip, not to wet my lips in below-freezing air.

But I can only be friends. I can't date a married guy.

It's in the works, he said straight at me. I promise.

In the hush of the woods, on that flat stretch, I skated up to him on my backcountry skis, skated half a body past him. Will you grab my water? I asked and tilted my head toward the side of my pack with my water bottle.

It's so beautiful! Words exploded out of me, then softer: I love the quiet. Makes me want to never downhill ski again. I glugged a quarter of my water bottle, wiped my mouth with the back of my glove.

We stood and listened to silence, sliced by heavy snow tumbling from branches. Mount Rainier's summit stretched to sky in the distance. I'd grown up in its shadow. Its distinctive saddle loomed all around Puget Sound.

Yes you are, he said, ice-blue eyes lasered on me. The mountain's beautiful, but you are more. You are my beauty.

And you're mine, I said, my whole body smiling. You're mine.

Before he was mine, he was someone else's. He had his own story of love and loss, and yet he offered his tenderness, his wholeness. How did Kent risk his heart with me?

He was almost divorced when Claire, his wife, died in a car crash on a mountain road. We were dating when she died a too-young death. He could have caged his heart. Instead, he gave it to me.

I'm so glad you're an experienced backpacker, Kent said as I snapped tent poles from their folded smallness to their bigness. Laced one pole through a tent peg. Waited for Kent to mirror what I'd done.

I'm glad you already love it, he said once we popped up the tent. This mini dome we'd sleep under for two nights.

I don't have to convince you it's great, he said, letting out air in a whale-sized puff.

Well, I'm happy you're already a backpacker too, I said and grinned.

Here was our conversation repeating. Him relieved he didn't need to teach me how to haul a backpack, snap together a tent, cook on a hand-sized stove, know the 10 essentials of backpacking, know how to use them. Survival skills I'd learned through grit and Never Give Up. Survival skills that were mine.

The woods rearranged me before Kent was even a possibility. Remagnetized me to my true north. I couldn't imagine being with someone who didn't love the outdoors.

Kent wore his thoughtful face. Deep thinker him. This man of sky and poetry. This man who wore feelings on his skin.

What is it?

He blinked. Turned a half turn away from me.

Claire wasn't a backpacker before me, he said.

Claire. His dead wife. He hardly talked about her except when I asked and even then, he'd sidestep my Are You Thinking of Claire? curiosity.

So I stopped on that day in the woods when he spoke Claire's name. Evergreen smells wrapped us. End of day sun, soft. Me with a tent pole mid-air, arched like it was hooked with a fish.

She came to love it, he said, checking the sky-blue sky. Our Yosemite trips were some of my favorites, he added. He scratched his beard at his jawline like he did.

I'm sorry, I said in almost a whisper.

My words punched at the base of my ribs and I knew they were true. I wouldn't wish a too-young death, not ever. I let the pole droop to the snow we'd packed hard with stomping feet.

Me too. He blew out a long breath. I still wanted her to be happy even if it wasn't with me.

I swigged a bellyful of mountain air, like I needed a side of courage to ask hard questions.

Was it hard for you to trust your heart with me?

He sucked his lips in a straight line. The tiny crop of beard hair below his bottom lip quivered.

I told myself I wouldn't trust anyone again around money, he said. And the ugly things before we filed for divorce.

I tapped my toes inside my boots.

Tree shadows stretched long and willowy. Dappled light shifted in patterns with the breeze. The close creek hummed its creek tune.

But then it was you—he looked into my eyes —and those walls I thought were sturdy kinda tumbled down. He paused. You know I trust you, right?

I do, I told him. I trust you too. Even with my own oceans of hurt, I did.

The breeze breezed harder.

Then: Hand me the bags, I said. I'll toss them in the tent.

I snapped the last snap of the tent's fly. Grinned into the papaya sky with its slipping down sun.

I had more questions.

I gotta ask you something else, I said, and made my big eyes even bigger.

Are you afraid I'll die too?

Before

Months before Claire's death, Kent and I were in our love swoon: hiking and concerts and wandering in Tower Books, Tower Records. There were mugs of coffee (me) and tea (him) with legs woven together while we read in bed with Sunday sun, with moonlight teasing the gauzy curtains. Add cross country and downhill skiing. Add mountain drives with Pink Floyd and Vivaldi. Add sex and love dives and kindness.

I soaked him in, content to let love unfold. Not so for Kent. This even-tempered man was in a rush when it came to me. Later I'd wonder if in some shadow self of him, he knew his life—our life—wasn't going to be creaky knees, fast cars for slow cars, and thumbing through memories.

Will you marry me? Kent asked one ski day. Words like a hiccup. No throat clearing. No blinking. No sticky palms. No one knee in snow or whatever other fantasy I'd fed from the days of playing wedding as a girl. We were at the base of a chair lift, clipping into skis, adjusting goggles.

What?

He grinned his grin that dug his chin groove and one dimple deeper. Grin that cranked up his aqua eyes.

Um, you're married, I said to his shrug.

Plus, I added with a shrug of my own.

I didn't finish that sentence.

I thought of the things I might say: Wait. What? Are you serious? We've only dated a month. You are super cute. You need to handle your divorce. Oh, I'd marry you for your eyes. No. Wait. What?

Almost divorced, he said while my thoughts side-barred.

Still married, I said with a hard stop. Then added: I'll race you to the lift line.

I skied off. My bumblebee-yellow ski jacket not quite zipped. I skated away to the end of the winding lift line, to give myself a moment. I'd struggled with even dating Kent since he was married. That promise my girl-self made: never be with a married man. That promise grew from my heartbreak of Dad cheating then abandoning our family. Not me. Uh-uh.

Blue sky day at Crystal Mountain, the same ski area where I'd learned to ski as a girl, when I took the ski bus up on Saturdays because I wanted to learn to ski and came from a family of not-ski-ers. I was 10 when I started catching the ski bus before sunrise on Saturdays, when I learned lessons bigger than how to snowplow, how to stop, eventually how to parallel ski. I learned to carry my own skis. To get to my lesson on time or they'd leave without me. To not lose my lift ticket. I learned freezing your 7-Up the night before keeps it cold for lunch (always a sack lunch back at the bus) and pops the end so it can't stand up. I learned if you don't slow yourself once you fall, you'll keep falling.

I mostly chased Kent on the slopes that ski day he asked me to marry him. His style: straighter and faster than mine. His navy-blue jacket flapping. Him on the verge of losing it. He loved skiing at the edge of danger. How fast could he go? How untamed? I hadn't skied since high school and was searching for my ski legs. Remembering all those instructions. The down-up-down—bend your knees/straighten/bend—of turning. Weight on the balls of your feet. Athletic stance. Point downhill, not up. And maybe my favorite: curling your toes in your boots won't help.

Partway through the day my body remembered the rush of zipping down the slopes, letting my skis run. Leaning in, not back. The body joy of swishing and turning and not turning. Red cheeks. Smile big as the sun.

We'd talk on the chair rides up. Words wrapped in cloud breath while we sat thigh to thigh while cold flushed our cheeks and made our noses run. He told me about a science experiment at a planetarium he'd been part of the summer before he came to Washington, the summer before we met. How he'd ridden his Norton motorcycle from his home in Pasadena, California to the site in Canada and back. How he'd decided on that coastal ride, the Pacific swirling and pounding on his left, then his right, that he needed a change since his wife wanted out of their marriage. He told me how perfect it was that the construction company where he worked as a project manager was running a new job in Washington and did he want to go?

This man with hypnotic eyes. With his slate-colored hair that made him look even older. My 22 to his 31 age gap felt like Saturn's 62 moons. I pictured the Game of Life board game: how he had a car and house and wife and a beard and a mortgage and dogs too, while I was straight out of college and bound for grad school. How all I owned was an old VW Bug and my skis from high school.

Plus, what would happen when this job finished? Would he go back to California? I scratched out my mental check list of pros and cons. We didn't add up. Or maybe we did.

Back in the lodge's parking lot we brushed ice and snow off skis and boots, peeled off parkas. He shrugged into his Pendleton wool jacket: large plaid in russet and pine squares with a creamy background. As I yanked a dry fleece over my head, he pulled me close. Arms circled bodies. My ear to his chest. His thunder heart boomed steady and true. His breath on the crown of my head. Puffs of breath in icy mountain air, like word bubbles.

He pulled back and soaked me in.

How about, I love you, he said.

This deep thinking man. A Caltech astronomer currently working as a project manager for a construction company. This man who loved celestial bodies and singing fake opera. Who loved the wonder of it all.

But.

Was he too old? Too married? Too grey? I thought my love person would resemble my first love, my high school to college love, who was shorter, darker, with bark-brown eyes like mine. What if I let my heart love him and he left? What if he stayed?

My ear pressed to his heart: the pound and swish of his fist-sized muscle.

Wrapped in a joy bolt. Pulse in my chest, four fingers below my collarbone, it beat, throbbed. This body spot: my truth pendulum pinged like an arcade game.

How about, I love you too.

The Once Broken Still Here hearts. Charcoal heart, a seared love note. Torn moss heart, tear like a lightning bolt. Heart-shaped scar on a tree limb. Pandora's Cluster in the night sky, a bruised heart shape at the center.

Rose red. Carmine. Chili pepper.

Corazon. Coeur. Herz. Kokoro.

Tiniest heart. Hummingbird heart: 1,260 heartbeats per minute. Weighs less than a feather. Big biggest heart: blue whale. Heart VW Beetle sized. Heart half-a-ton sized.

After

I idled in my idling car in the driveway of Emily's office. Squinted past evergreen trees at Mount Rainier's peak. I stared down the digital clock. Counted seconds between the minute flips. Scratched my itchy palms. Poked at the tiny fluid-filled stress bumps scattered in the valleys of my fingers. Told myself to call the dermatologist even though I knew I wouldn't.

I tracked four women crossing from sunshine to inside, to the waiting area with a pot of brewed Mr. Coffee, Styrofoam cups, and Coffee Mate always prepped.

Two blondes. Two brunettes. In heels and flats. In tennis shoes. In slacks and jeans, jackets and sweatshirts. Clean hair and make-up too. They were chatting, laughing even. Did I have the right group? Yes. Tuesday at 11. That's what Emily told me.

I swallowed hard. Chest-pressed ribs. Stones on chest. An old-fashioned term for depression.

Let's go, I said, checking my eyes in the rearview mirror. This slice of my face: half nose, eyes, half wrinkled brow. My eyes matte. No catch-light. I almost couldn't see my tiger's eye; this tiny fleck outside my iris that Grandma Sally used to tell me meant I could see what many don't. Was it still there or had I lost it too?

Before

Do you see it? Kent asked, adjusting the focus on his telescope, his fancy one we toted outside on cloudless nights when the stars salted the sky.

I squinted my closed eye harder.

The outer shape looks like a skull, he said, while I tucked my interrupting hair behind my ear and soaked in the night sky.

See the rose shape in the dense part?

It's gorgeous, I whispered. My mouth sticky dry. It's so faint, I said. I almost can't see it.

Rose in a skull. Skull cradling rose. Beauty and death helixed together.

I knew you'd like that one, he said, all grin.

It reminds me of visiting the catacombs in Paris, he said, and how much you loved the tunnels of bones and walking with the dead. How you loved the orange and purple light orbs you saw around us.

We breathed for a moment inside memory. Feet scuffing dirt. The cool of underground, tingling our skin. The beauty of walking with the remains of over six million people while our hearts beat on. Reverence for the dead, for a culture honoring death, sculpting art with bones. The entrance sign: *Arrête! C'est ici l'empire de la Mort.* Stop! This is the Empire of the Dead.

I loved it there, I said. It felt holy.

I scrunched up my closed eye and looked harder. This skull is hard to see, I said. And I thought again of the skulls that lined the bone walls in the catacombs. Skulls as fringe, as embellishment. Skulls in the shapes of crosses embedded in bone walls.

I'll show you pictures of it. It's clearer in photographs.

I love the skull and rose together, I said, soft. Squishy feeling in my chest, the shores of my heart all melty.

The many sides of you, Kent said and wrapped me in his arms. Even through his down jacket I could hear the echo of his ocean heart. The bass beat of it.

Just look to the left of Orion the Hunter to find it. That's where the rose and skull live.

I pointed to Rosette Nebula and drew my name in the stars: Annie, Annie, Annie like I did when I was a girl, marking my place.

I might need a map, I told him.

You won't. You'll always have me.

We stargazed in puffy down parkas zipped up to our ears. He showed me Cassiopeia, Sagittarius (There you are.) He told me again how we are made of galactic dust, how we leave dust maps. The stars in us. Us in the stars.

After he died, I forgot star magic.

I forgot so many things.

After

I didn't want to put on my fucking shoes and go to the widows' group.

But I did.

After three months of twice weekly just-me therapy, I agreed to visit and maybe (See the maybe. Terror filled my shoes.) join the young widows: all women under 40 with kids. Me, the youngest. Jake, the youngest, youngest.

You're ready, Therapist Emily coaxed while I chomped my bottom lip. The bridge of my nose throbbed. Hard. Tears broke the shore of me.

You are, she repeated while I wiped my face.

Here's what I couldn't say to Emily then: How I wanted to stay in the dark. Cocoon myself with Depression, my tea sipping, crying companion. How I wanted to stay anchored on the bottom of the ocean in the blackest black. How I didn't want to go to therapy. How I had to go. How I didn't want to be in the cemetery club. How I longed to bury my busted self and ignore her. My first therapy appointment I told kind-eyed Emily: I'm here for Jake. Just Jake. I don't care about me.

I have this vision of him grown, telling his therapist: My dad died before I was born. Then my mom went crazy.

I can't have that.

Help me be enough of a mom, I said, busting into tears, wrapping my arms around my ribs and squeezing, like I could tether untethered-me.

After Kent died I'd lie on my bed. Sobbing monsoon tears. Skinless. Muscles and nerves pulsing. Tears flooding my ear scoops. Stones on my chest. An avalanche of boulders. Breathing through a straw, like I was some drying death mask waiting for the plaster to harden. I'd hear the tick of my heart, and in the anguish of me, beg for silence. I didn't want to hear heart or breath. I didn't want to be sound. I'd feel the up and down behind tired ribs and wonder how my heart pumped all broken. Even when I held my breath, praying: Stop. Will you fucking stop.

My heart beat—pumping, pushing, and pulling me with it.

Emily told us you were coming, one of the widows said when I slumped through the waiting area and straight into Emily's office with everyone picking chairs, our knees too close, coffee and spearmint gum breath tumbling together.

My eyes flitted from the comfy saddle brown leather chairs to the textiles on the walls to the two-story dollhouse and doll family to the bookshelves jammed with self-help books. Tiny glances at the women: at the blondes and brunettes. At four women who looked like women I'd see in the grocery store, at the community college where I taught, at a coffee shop, in a book group. A circle of women. They looked, um, normal. Like they'd showered and brushed their hair. Like they hadn't been bawling in their cars like me.

My skin numbed like I'd plunged in the icy Skookumchuck River at our family ranch. Was this the right group?

This group was a group already. I—snap—turned into my second-grade self at a new school: the new girl with the wrong clothes, wrong lunchbox, with a spirally stomach, with a mouth full of questions locked away. The new girl whose parents were getting divorced. The only second grader in my class with split parents. Broken home. That was the term then.

And here I felt broken again.

Widow circle. While they named their names—Liz, Maddie, Sarah, and Beth—I wished for name tags. Blondes and brunettes. Heart attack husbands and accident husbands. I grouped them as 1) who was with their husband when he died and 2) who wasn't. Quick deaths. Slow deaths. How I was like them, how I wasn't.

Before

Kent and I twined in the cooling end of day. Fingers pressed spines, the braille of us, through his Pendleton wool jacket, through my charcoal winter coat that tugged in the front, snug across my belly, swollen with life. My ear cupped to his chest, to his boom, bump heart. The pulse of him through my fingertips. His fire heated my belly, arms, throat, hands.

We'd just left my sixth-month pregnancy checkup with our fish boy stretching and swimming, backstroking in his private pond.

I never thought I could love you more, I said as we listened to our boy's high-octane heartbeat. But I do.

We grinned giddy when Dr. H said: What a good solid heart. I can already tell your boy has a good heart.

We rolled names around in our Almost Parent mouths like watermelon Jolly Ranchers and wondered if we'd like a hard name like Carl or a soft one like Joel.

How about Norton, Kent said and wiggled his eyebrows like he did when he was teasing.

Sure, I laughed. Name our boy after your favorite motorcycle.

Almost Mom and Almost Dad laced in a hug. On the cusp of couple to family. In the later afternoon of a winter day. Slate sky inking to pewter.

He was mountain bound, a night of night skiing. I was home bound, grading a double stack of student papers bound, too belly round to ski bound.

I'm chasing daylight, he said as he kissed the crown of my head, as his breath fogged in the winter-cold parking lot.

As our arms uncoupled, my gut cramped. Air jackknifed in ribs, in the knot of me.

I pulled back and studied my husband.

I pulled back to breathe.

Kent. Wet-concrete grey hair. Light brown beard with spice streaks. The bluest eyes I'd ever seen or ever will.

He kissed me again as the winter sky bruised up. I smelled the outdoors on him: snow and sky, wind and ice, stars and galaxies and black holes too.

Don't go, I almost said through my pin-sized throat, as a thrumming climbed my windpipe.

Something's not right, I almost said.

Words crouched in my mouth.

I already knew what he'd say.

You can't live your life in a box. His favorite motto. I could have put it on his headstone. He said it when we quit our jobs and traveled Europe for two months. He said it when he handed me a helmet and I climbed on the back of his Norton motorcycle. He said it when we parasailed and the man strapping me into my harness warned: You barely make the weight requirement and it's windy. We'll probably need to drop you in the ocean instead of the dock. Still want to go? He said it when he cranked up Pink Floyd's "Wish You Were Here."

Your anthem? I'd say and he'd grin.

You can't live your life in a box.

Instead of begging him to stay, I gulped my scared.

He kissed the crown of my head as my body shivered.

He pressed against my lunar belly with: I love you.

I'll see you late tonight, he said.

I'll slip in beside you while you sleep your crazy deep sleep.

You won't even know I was gone.

I want to stop right here. Pry open words and sentences. Anchor my feet on one sentence, my hands on the line above, turn my body into a wedge and bust open this space to the Before. For years I wished I could stall out here, warn us. Stop!

That's not his story.

That's not my story.

After

Before the widows' group, there was just Emily.

Have you called Emily? Jake's pediatrician asked again after he weighed and measured my three-week-old boy. Dr. D was the attending doctor in the hospital: pure tender and kindness with Jake and me and my family (I see a lot of family with you, he had said during hospital rounds. But I haven't seen a husband, a partner, he added. Is there a partner? And I burst into tears.) The first office visit, after I'd written Dead Dad on Jake's forms (and of course Dr. D asked how he died: Was there an illness?) he told me about Therapist Emily, who ran a support group of young widows.

Please give her a call, he said, and wrote her name and number on the back of one of his cards. She's easy to talk to.

I jammed the card in my coffee-colored quilted diaper bag, somewhere near wipes or a clean/dirty T-shirt, and forgot about it.

I'm going to have Emily call you, he said as he scribbled notes in Jake's chart. This man whose body was all bones and edges. Whose voice was soft.

My stomach twitched. Then didn't. What therapist calls a person if they don't call first?

How's Jake's weight? I asked, my toes talking to each other in my Converse tennies.

He looks great, he said, and grinned at baby Jake in my arms. The warmth of Jake across my belly. His unmarked baby skin, creamy and smooth. The comfort of how we puzzled together. He smelled like baby powder and goodness.

Let's keep up the weight checks, Dr. D said. He smiled his bright teeth smile and nodded twice. Tiny flecks of silver by his ears glinted, like a sprinkle of after-party confetti.

He's still a little low on the weight scale, he said. We'll do weekly checks for now. Just to be safe.

Safe. A zing jolt of something jolted me. Everything felt unsafe in my upside-down world. Me. Walking around skinless. All my nerve endings taller than me, rubbed raw.

Are you okay? Dr. D asked.

I wanted to be new mom okay-and-not-okay. I wanted nursing (Is he getting enough? Do I have enough?) and sleeping-not-sleeping (Does anyone sleep in this new baby/solo mom equation?) and Did he poop (Today? When?) to be my big worries. Not widow worries that taunted in the dark of me. Everything stitched with missing Kent. My inner voice on loud: *You're futureless. Kent doesn't get to have any of this. You're losing your memories too.* Double down with practical worries: *Teaching part-time on two campuses barely feeds you. You screwed up not having life insurance. What if you lose your home? How will you care for Jake and yourself?*

I didn't want this liminal space that felt like an Escher staircase drawing where up is down and down is down and Where am I in the Labyrinth? What's real anymore?

Not this cauldron of feels I could and couldn't name.

I wished I could go back to Numb Land. Burrow in a blanket fort. Forever.

Bad question, Dr. D said to my silence. Me, swallowing tears before they swallowed me.

Of course you're not okay. I'm so sorry.

Then.

Can I do anything for you?

All I wanted was what no one could do: bring Kent back. In the early time I begged for another 40 years, a fullish life span. Then I pleaded to take whatever time I had left and split it with him. Lately I longed for five minutes. Just let me hold him one more time, bubble him up with love words: I love you I love you I love you.

I couldn't voice my want.

My throat heated. That trap door I imagined at the base of my throat, slammed hard.

I pulled my mouth in a straight line and shook my head *no*.

I did what I did. Focused on Jake to stay in my body, to slow the What If I Break Even More spiral. Bent one of his tiny arms then the other into his onesie with the half-inch-tall blueberry-blue bears on parade. Then his jammies with the drawstring closure. Swaddled him in more blue (a flannel blanket, mini-burrito style), tucked him in his carrier, covered his sweet head with his soft cotton hat with a duckling-yellow pompom.

I'll see you next week, Dr. D said, tapping the door with his pen.

I'm worried about you, he added, like a footnote, before he stepped out of the exam room. I think you'll like Emily. She's easy to talk to.

Who's the drinker in your family? Emily asked in our first private session. I felt a rush of shame. When I stalled, she said, We'll get to that later.

My dad, I blurted. I didn't add his brother, his dad. I didn't add cousins.

But he quit when I was 14, I said in a rush and felt that slurry of shame slosh from gut, swirl through stomach, esophagus, to the skinny of my throat.

A lot happens before 14, she said, and I almost barfed.

A gut of shame. More. A body of shame. Habanero hot and slimy. I didn't know then how shame was sutured in my DNA through generations of drinkers. I didn't understand this complex tapestry of being raised with drinkers and then an undoing grief.

Molten insides. Volcano rage hissed and bubbled. I'd ranted at the accident, the messed-up timing, the unfairness, the cosmos. When Emily asked if I was angry at Kent, I denied it. He didn't want to die. Who could be mad at him?

Me. The one he left behind. Me with my mass of hurt that had no beginning and no end. Me who couldn't speak my grief, so instead I lost my words.

Raised by Vodka Dad and Depressed Mom, I'd mastered holding truths behind my teeth. Even when rage burned a hole in me. Even when that hole turned to ulcer when I was eight.

I first learned Abandoned when I was about seven. With Dad leaving. With Mom fading to a line drawing of herself. With me packing my girl suitcase to go to Dad's. The plaid suitcase with the red piping and the big fake brass buckle. I'd pretend I was Edith in *The Lonely Doll*. Edith with her blonde hair, straight bangs, gingham dress, Mary Jane shoes. Edith who goes to live with the Bear family.

I read *The Lonely Doll* endlessly, curled on a blanket Grandma Sally gave me, secreted in my bedroom closet where I made a reading corner just my size. Light tumbled in through the louvered slats and made stripes across my legs. Dust mites tumbled in the V of my flashlight when sunlight greyed.

While my book-loving mom carted us to the Book Nook Bookstore and the library, while she bought me a collection of *Peanuts* and *Little Bear* books one at a time, she refused to buy *The Lonely Doll*, no matter how I begged.

It's not right, she'd say. That girl without a family, living with bears.

Since I couldn't own it, I checked it out at the library on repeat.

The librarian with her tiny half-glasses and too-tight belt—always with a crumpled Kleenex jammed in the waistband—would ask me when she'd see my name filling up the checkout card: You're sure there's not another book you'd like?

I'd shake my head.

I only wanted Edith.

I *was* Edith.

Edith who packed her black-and-red plaid suitcase.

Mine included:

Flannel nightgown

Jeans

T-shirt

Carter undies and undershirts

Brush

Toothbrush

A book

Sketch pad and pencils, erasers

A marble or two

Maalox

You have your Maalox? Mama asked, her heels clicking against the cold slate floor. Her voice spilled down the long too-white hall. Maalox. Chalky pills I chewed with every meal in silence. No one would tell me why I had to eat them. I asked.

You'll just worry, Mama said, Dad said.

Didn't they know I worried about everything? Was I dying? Why'd Dad leave? Was he coming back? Was it my fault? If I didn't count my steps from the front door to the kitchen, to my room, back down the hall and outside, if I didn't make words come out in groups of fives and tens that I drummed and drummed on my fingertips, would something bad happen? Something worse?

What was wrong with me?

I squeezed my eyes shut and saw my insides: this lava-grey ball of goo, with streaks of pink and red veins, tiny, jagged teeth, tentacles that stretched across my tummy, tentacles that smelled like a lifejacket put away wet.

You're growing an alien! my older sister Lisa said when I'd hold my stomach.

Did you pack Maalox? Mama asked if I didn't answer.

A little girl suitcase full of little girl things. Plus Maalox. This girl suitcase I never unpacked at Dad's. Where I kept my things zipped up, ready for a quick escape.

The first and third weekends of each month, my sisters and I dragged our suitcases from Mama's house to Dad's car, from Dad's car to Mama's house. I did my best to carry it, but it smacked my shins and I mostly dragged it. Behind us in the house, Mama sobbed, her crying tendrils searching for us.

And there was Dad. Parked at the curb with the motor running. The years clicked by in cars: red Mustang, blue Thunderbird, red Cadillac, white Cadillac, white Mercedes.

Before

Do you want the top two drawers and I'll take the bottom two? Kent asked and wiggled his eyebrows.

I was 24, almost married. Saying Hi to the ocean on the Washington coast.

The mouth of his suitcase flopped open on the bed. Socks and boxers in one hand. He yanked open the third drawer down.

Huh?

You take the top, he said and laughed, twinkle in his eyes like sun on a lake.

You can have them all, I said, eyeing my suitcase on the luggage stand. Black soft-sided Samsonite with a brass zipper.

We're here for a week, he said, sweeping his arms wide, game show host style. He pointed past the open window to the roaring ocean and seersucker-blue sky. My skin tasted sun and sand.

Don't you wanna unpack?

A twitch in my gut. Ancient snake ache.

I shook my head.

Could I tell this honey man I never unpack? This man who grew up in the home his father built before he was born and his still-married parents still lived there, kept his boy room in boyhood with model planes and science awards. This man whose roots were solid as a western hemlock.

I get all the drawers? he asked as I opened the windows and surf sounds flooded in.

Before

You studied the sky with your kid lens. Your telescope drawn from its cardboard box with your name in pressed block letters: Kent Neuberger. You claimed the sky. The wonder of night.

You studied the sky at Caltech, at the planetarium in Griffith Park. Dense stars. Constellations. Black holes. White dwarfs. Double stars. Meteors. Milky Way. Nebulas. Novas. The waxing and waning of the moon—in all its plumpness, slivers, crests.

You studied the sky, the summer before we met, at a planetarium in Canada. The summer you stepped away from your marriage before me, into the night sky, through a black hole and back.

You studied the night sky. The two of us flopped on loam, on grass, on my favorite blanket Grandma Sally gave girl-me. You traced shapes: Sirius, Canis Major, Cassiopeia.

Do you feel big or small? you asked me.

What?

Do you feel big or small? When you wonder at the stars.

Big. Like I'm a part of it, I said as you folded your body around mine.

Where's the archer? I asked. That Sagittarius sign that is me, squared.

You're right there, you said, your lean finger tracing shapes, connecting star dots.

You're in the stars. The stars in you.

You drew infinity in the night sky. That sideways figure eight.

It's a love loop, you said. It never ends.

I love you times infinity, you said from the start, you said in the short and wide five years that were ours.

You studied the sky. You in the rib of the moon.

You saw you there when I still wanted you here.

Before

You're only as fast as your slowest hiker, Luke said and made his winky face, squinting under the Wyoming sky. The other two instructors and 14 students slung their packs back on as soon as I reached the group, as soon as I was ready to ditch my ogre of a pack—that weighed 60 (SIXTY!) pounds—and take a break. Soon as Luke and I slogged up to the group they were Packs On, Ready, Go, Gone.

This group of students and instructors on a National Outdoor Leadership School (NOLS) 30-day wilderness course in the Wyoming mountains. Students as young as 15, as old as 30-something. I was 22, wishing I'd done it when I was younger—no—more fit, wishing my body wasn't 30 pounds extra and a master smoker.

Still, I followed my impulse. Followed my heart to the woods. Maybe losing me in the backcountry was a way back to me. Me who'd gotten muddled performing daughter, sister, girlfriend, friend. Who am I when I'm just me? How do I stand? Move? What's the sound of my true voice?

So I picked this extreme thing: hiking 10 and more hours a day through the deep woods, no trails, no signposts. Then I found out part of who I was: the slowest hiker. Any romantic ideas about trekking through the woods, singing Cat Stevens, swimming in shafts of sunshine, were squashed by my bully pack that I had to take everywhere.

After

Emily's cozy office: nutmeg-colored leather couch and side chairs, red accent pillows, oak coffee table, Kleenex, packed bookshelves, a doll house and dolls and stuffed animals, two large house plants in baskets, textiles on the walls, black-and-white Ansel Adamsy mountain photos, extra Kleenex. Cozy. Sit. Talk. You're safe here.

Still. I wanted to run. What was I afraid of? My deep fear of being judged? Not grieving right? Afraid of shedding grief layers? If I let grief go, would I have to let Kent go too?

Who else? Emily asked in the long pause as she looked around the group of widows.

I shifted in the leather chair and it made an old saddle sound.

I'm Liz, said one of the brunettes. Did you go to Stadium?

I nodded.

I think you know my sister, Liz went. When I read about your husband in the paper, I asked her. She remembers you.

Liz waited a beat to my silence.

I'm sorry about your husband, she said, soft.

A chaplain woke me in the middle of the night. I knew Kent was dead when I pressed baby belly to the cool metal door, when I spied out the fish-eyed peephole at the white rectangle on the stranger's collar. I wouldn't let him in.

If I kept him out, what he came to say didn't happen. Before and after moments.

Cusps.

Cusps: a point of transition between two different states. In architecture, cusp is a projecting point between small arcs in Gothic designs. In sky, cusp is the pointy points of a crested moon. In anatomy: a pocket in the wall of the heart that fills and empties.

When I did let the grey haired, droopy-eyed chaplain step from there to here, it felt like drowning, ears on fire, words—Your husband died in a car accident—muffled in my underwater world. When he asked, Who can you call? I said, No one.

One of the widows scooted closer, her chair scraping the linoleum.

The wad in my throat bloomed like a soggy sea sponge, squishy to my ears.

Words tunneled in my spongy throat. What was wrong with me? I'd been a talker and then Kent died and my words went underground.

I didn't have language for hard feelings. I padded feelings, buried the dark ones, camouflaged with grace or humor when I was being my Grown-in-a-Fucked-Up-Family self, when I was performing Fine Girl (I'm fine I'm fine I'm fine) I'd learned to be in the house of buried truths—where Dad's moving out a suitcase at a time was never explained—where sometimes we'd wake up on a Saturday and he'd be in bed with Mom, and sisters and I would shriek joy and everything felt brighter until he'd leave again and sleep with someone else. When I was sevenish, I remember some-one gushing (What a beautiful family!) one Sunday church day when we were a family of five, when sisters and I were scrubbed and shiny from our patent leather shoes to our tiny patent purses and my stomach lurched. I almost threw up. Even though every cell of me wanted beautiful family to be true, my belly knew it wasn't.

How'd you know that so young? my sis asked years later when we stayed in the wrinkleless guest room at Dad's, when we stared at the popcorn ceiling in the hush of dark and shared secrets. My body knew, I said. The not-rightness. It's why I grew that ulcer.

Slumped in my favorite saddle-colored chair in Emily's office, the pinch where I had worn a ponytail for years pinched harder.

My mouth tasted like I'd sucked on a penny then scarfed a sleeve of Saltines racing a 30-second timer.

Liz crossed her foot up on her knee. Tugged on the hem of her sweatshirt.

She'd be the one I remembered from the start. The one I'd be friends with over 30 years later even though I didn't know it in that moment.

Well, Liz started. We've had a week—

She talked about her kids, how they missed AJ (their dad), and how that broke her heart. How her own missing him (and she missed him huge) felt puny next to her kids' longing, next to their fears that she'd die too. She told how they tucked her love notes under her door when everything was too much and she hid in her bedroom and sobbed.

I just want to be little again, she said. I got out an old snow globe. It's on the mantle to remind me how things were simple—or seemed simple—when I was a girl.

I stretched fingers I'd squeezed to numb. Smoothed my thumb over fingernail dents I'd carved in my palms.

I wanted to be little too. Romp at our family ranch. Ride horses. Pretend to drive the rusted-out pickup truck while my best cousin and I plotted road trips to Tennessee. I wanted my biggest worries to be getting caught sitting on the fence of the bull pen or facing down the timer at dinner for being a slow eater or talking my way out of a wooden spoon spanking.

I wanted to say, Me too, but the words gummed in my sea sponge throat.

The women in the room spoke their grief stories, their Dead Husband Stories. Their pain stuck to my skin. Their pain didn't stick to my skin. Two dead husbands by heart attacks. One a runner. One a soccer player. A third dead husband buried alive in a construction accident when a trench caved in. By the time they dug him out, he was dead, suffocated: wrongful death suit. Sarah brushed something invisible off her pant leg as she talked about taking her check to the bank and the young teller, not knowing, said, Boy I wish I were depositing this check, and Sarah said, No, you don't. Not if you knew how it came to me.

Breath trapped in the soft where collarbones meet. I—snap—cried. No warm-up. No throat tickle. No eye twitch. No thick feeling in the cave of my mouth. All the ways my body signaled tears. All the ways I'd felt since I was a crying girl. I wanted words. Could I at least have said I was sorry? But my word burrowed in the coils of me.

Then Beth's husband, a police officer: shot. Died in the line of duty. He clicked his belt, straightened his badge, kissed her goodbye with, I'll see you tonight. When the front door closed behind him, she worried, like she did every day. She told herself he'd be fine, he always came home. Except he didn't.

My gut sizzled listening to her. I imagined its pinky slimy self all orange red, the shade of burning steel. Charcoal where fire had already torched me.

Words. Where were my fucking words? I wanted to say, I'm sorry. I wanted to say, My husband died suddenly too, in a car crash on a mountain road on his way to go night skiing. Oh, and he was speeding.

I can't tell you the details of the accident because I wasn't there. No. I can't tell you because my insides will leak out in the telling.

Sitting almost knees to knees with these women, Kent's wish to ski more before Jake was born seemed wrong and selfish next to the police-officer widow's story, next to all the stories. It didn't matter that I knew not to weigh pain against itself, weigh mine to theirs, theirs to mine. I did it anyway.

Annie? Emily asked.

Fear wrapped my heart. Shame pinged my spine. Everything about me felt ugly. I was scared my voice would be dragon voice. Holding it in felt safer than letting it out.

Want to introduce yourself?

Before

The muscle boys were the fastest of 15 students. The muscle boys—15- and 16-year-olds—two, maybe three of them with shallow faces, walled eyes. One turned out to be my tent mate, declaring—before we even flipped for who carried the tent and who carried the fly—I don't want to be here. Parents made me.

The muscle boys slung their 60-pound packs on like school bags. I envied their ease when I buckled under my pack that knocked me sideways, tipped me over if I bent too far at the waist.

I thought I was dying for a break but, of course, I wasn't dying. I was 22 and able-bodied. After those 30 days in the wilderness, I took up running and weight training and shapeshifted into stunning shape. No longer the slowest. But on that hot dusty trail, I was.

Fingers curled on my belt clip, aching to dump my beasty pack that dug into hipbones. Bruises soon. Layered bruises turned leathery after a week or two. Ear-pounding breath hard and edgy.

Swamped in sweat. Feet on fire. Hot spots on my feet blooming to blisters.

I'll grab your water, Luke said and freed it from a side pocket. We gotta keep going. Keep your pack on. The group is already ahead of us.

Did I cry? Maybe. Maybe when that first stop turned out not to be a stop.

Done much backpacking? he asked as I glugged water. This third instructor, keeping pace with slug-me.

Some, I told him and wiped my mouth with the back of my hand. American kid in Europe like some college kids. On and off trains. Sleeping in the aisles. Adventure my oxygen. My 20-pound pack (20 pounds tops, maybe less) was mostly a prop that went with my Eurail pass from youth hostels to trains to youth hostels. My maroon Jan Sport pack only got weighty in Greece where I bought souvenirs: religious icons with gold frames (Gold paint of course. Me, a college student on a budget.) for my Greek grandparents, a clay pot patterned with a Greek key design for Mom, Greek flags in T-shirts and coffee mugs for everyone else. My heritage, my Greekness all lit when I swooned over the beauty of the islands, the colors, the blue sky and sea, the lemon sun, when I wept at the thought of my grandparents fleeing Greece two generations ago. What they left behind. What they carried with them.

Hmmm, Luke hummed as he eyed the dusty path, wide enough for two feet, the evergreens that were still tall at that elevation. Sun pricked green branches. Sunbeams. Cathedral light. Soon we'd be beyond paths, above the tree line, climbing above 10,000 feet.

Ready?

I got this, I silently told myself. *Let's go.*

I wouldn't call it hiking, not yet. More the speed of banana slugs and giant tortoises and sea anemones. My northwest sensibilities tuned my heart, even in the dry Wyoming mountains.

Luke jammed my water bottle back in its side pocket, angling me a little sideways. I stumbled and caught myself before I tipped over.

My sister's going on this crazy backpacking course, my younger sister Jan said, low, into the pink princess phone in her room, worry inking her words. Me in the hall, quiet outside her door.

Of course I've asked her why, she told her friend on the other end.

Yeah, I've said it's a horrible idea. Thirty days in the woods with no toilets, no beds, no toilet paper. Gross.

Bears? Geez, I've asked that too. And what about her period? Don't bears like blood? She just shrugs, says she doesn't know, says she's gotta go.

Here's the truth. I didn't have a good answer to my family asking why. Or even a bad answer. I didn't grow up in a backpacking family. I grew up with our family ranch where I romped outdoors on the weekends and summers, where I rode horses, fished, teased chickens, swam in the river, read and drew and painted in the shade of giant trees. Where I didn't have to bathe every day or wear dresses and ruffled anklets or crisp ribbons in my braids. Where I got to be feral. But we didn't hike in my girlhood. Or tent sleep. Or cook with a stove the size of a softball. Or haul water from creeks to campsites.

The tug to go was bigger than everyone else's doubts. Bigger than my mountain-sized doubts.

After

Annie, want to introduce yourself? Emily repeated as I sat in the widows' circle.

Sandpaper tongue, the ceiling of my mouth, my teeth. I swallowed hard. Swallowed my uncertainty.

I'm Annie, I said, and the blondes and brunettes bobbed their heads in *Go on. We're Listening.*

My husband died in a car accident.

I wanted to say he was alone. Crashed his car on black ice on the way to go night skiing. I wanted to say I was pregnant. I wanted to say I'm a single mom to my darling boy.

I wanted.

Me: dizzy, untethered. A tangle of feelings wadded up with duct tape. I breathed deep and steady to stay rooted. I shook my head *No* to Emily's invitation to say more.

Who can you think of? the chaplain asked.

I won't leave until someone gets here, he said and scrubbed the edges of his graphite eyes.

Me underwater.

Ears flooded as the river gushed by.

Icy skin. Lungs packed with curing concrete.

Heart blazed. Black fire. Sizzling at the edges of a fire ring with the river swirling above.

When I was six, I was stuck in an orange life jacket since I wasn't a real swimmer. It crowded my ears and smelled like river and shadows and something deep and sour. One boiling summer day at the swimming hole on our family ranch—cousins in the water, my aunt with her Jackie O sunglasses reading *Valley of the Dolls* on the shore, her Marlboro Red cigarette ash curving into a *J*—I peeled off the soggy too-big life jacket. Peeled it from skin with the certainty that I could swim as good as the big kids.

My big sis yelled, Whatcha doing?

Maybe she yelled, Wait! Stop! as I curled my toes into bird claws, put my hands together like praying and flopped my girl-self into the churning river.

When I sank straight down, lungs burning, when I screamed underwater, when I pushed off the slimy river bottom, pushed hard, when I broke the surface, squinted at sun before dropping again with all the weight of me. I swallowed more river, pure and sludgy. I must have passed out.

I woke up coughing then throwing up, water dripping off my aunt's curly dark hair, her normal soft face not-soft, more like a fox with darting eyes. Her voice high and tight. Her words: What were you thinking?

Who'd like to start then? Emily asked in her maple voice with a raspy timber, that undertone of East Coast poking through.

I dug my nails into my palms. I could feel eight crescents whiting up in the flesh of me.

A blonde (maybe Maddie) brushed crumbs off her skirt or rubbed them in. Hard to tell. She races here during lunch, she told me. Eats in the car. Next time she'll rub egg salad from the corners of her mouth but the smell of egg and mayo will linger.

I'm single and going on a date, Maddie announced, leaning in so far I thought she'd tip over.

My thoughts spun: *What the fuck? Single? Date?* My head squeezed where a ponytail would be if my hair were longer. Whites of my eyes circled my irises. Brows tented. What the fuck. What-TheFuck. What. The. Fuck.

I was here for oceans of tears: mix in hurt, anger, regret. I was here for stories about broken dishes, burned lingerie. How they slept during the day and couldn't sleep at night. How they ate too much. How they didn't eat. How they drank too much. Or didn't. How they couldn't see past today or even this minute. How they missed their husbands with every body cell.

Not moon-faced, curly-headed Maddie announcing independence from grief. Single. Dating.

Holy fuck of everything.

When? asked a brunette (Sarah maybe) in a cocoa-colored pantsuit with a pale pink blouse. A high ruffle framed her kind face.

This weekend. I'll tell you all about it next time. Maddie with her elfin grin and Raphael cherub cheeks.

I hated Maddie. I didn't feel inspired, like I could be Maddie someday. I felt pissed. Resentful.

I eyed the others, wondering what kind of I'm single bullshit would spill from their mouths.

I breathed deep and drummed fingers to thighs, studying these women, secretly wishing to see a little of me reflected. They looked so . . . Regular. Hair fixed. Makeup. Clothes ironed and matching. Not me in the Grab What's in the Dryer or Wipe the Baby Crud Off and Go. Even with fall pressing on, I didn't wear socks. One less thing to wash.

I hid my fists. Pressed nails into skin, in the map of me with my two marriage lines, with my bean-shaped pink scar at the headwater of those lines. I wanted grievers. Widows struggling to breathe. Widows whose biggest accomplishment might have been turning off the bedside lamp before passing out or putting soap in the dishwasher.

I wanted the Widowed and Fucked group.

Who can you call? the chaplain asked again, palms pressed into the saffron-colored kitchen counter. His hands grey from the cold.

Who?

My relationships with my parents were prickly. I'd twisted and shaped an imaginary barbed wire fence between us—see-through with spiky warnings—as I forged my own identity. A me separate from the unlucky parts of my childhood: their epic divorce, Dad's drinking, Mom's depression. Our family motto: Everything Looks Better on a Silver Platter.

We were close if we kept our truths on low volume.

And yet. I knew they'd show up. We gagged hurts to be there when being there mattered. Even with me wrestling with what does Family First mean now that Kent was my first family, my parents and sisters wouldn't hesitate to be the heartlines we'd always been.

Do you have family nearby? the chaplain asked, his TicTac breath turning sour.

My tongue wandered to a back molar.

Bare toes beat against the fake brick linoleum.

Snow inched up the deck rail just past the kitchen window.

I wished I'd put on socks.

You have to call someone, he said.

All my air trapped between collarbones that were icing up. Lungs petrifying.

My sisters. I loved them hard. And if I called them first, my parents would be pissed.

I rolled my hand over my belly. The tiny kick of a tiny baby part pressed into my fingertips.

A neighbor? he asked when I wedged myself in the corner of the kitchen counter.

I silently willed him to leave. *Get out.*

If I didn't call anyone, if I could get him gone, none of this would be true.

Do you know your neighbor's number?

Fine, I half-hissed. All pissy like this whole mess was this guy's fault.

I picked up that lead phone and called my mom and stepdad. Then dialed my dad. I said words through the moss in my mouth.

We'll be right there, Mom said.

Call your sisters, Dad said.

Call them now, he said to my silence.

Fifteen minutes later, Mom and my stepdad J. showed up in trench coats and hats and flannel pajamas and clogs and boots. My sisters and brother-in-law came next, stamping snow off tennis shoes under the fuzzy porch light. They wrapped me in arms and disbelief, holding me when all my form melted.

Dad came first thing in the morning, joining our sobbing gang that had watched night turn to day in the longest night of my life.

What do you need? Dad asked before he drove over.

Kent to live a little in a box, I said, my voice a question.

Oh, he could never do that. And I'd give you that if I could, he added, his voice trailing off like smoke.

Anything else? We listened to daughter/dad breath. Umbilical of silence.

He was a good man, Dad said.

I choked on *was.*

Tears flooded my throat. Swamped my ears. Burst out. This gush of thunder tears that split me.

I'm on my way, he said. *I'll be right there.*

In my blackest black my family wrapped me up. A love wrap. A We're Here wrap. A We've Got You wrap. Like the messy orange life jacket from girlhood. Too big and just right.

Wrapped. Snapped. Snugged.

After

In the new, raw grief days my words, my family's words were clipped: It's horrible. I can't believe it. How? Why? It's the worst thing imaginable. The worst. Sobbing and nose blowing and silence punched with sighs and goddamnits and shits.

No fuck at first. Fuck me came later. All the fucks: What the fuck is this? Who the fuck cares? I give no fucks. I'm all out of fucks. All. Out. Of. Fucks. Fresh out. This is fucked. The fuck of it all. Fuck as noun and verb and adjective and adverb too because I didn't fucking care what the fuck people thought was fuckerly right or fuckerly wrong about grief.

Once I stopped pretending I could navigate the blackest black, everything started with fuck.

Fuck trying to get grief right.

Are you okay? people asked.
Are you getting better?
If you need anything, just ask.
I think about you all the time.

I wanted to make little business cards, Times font, off-white sturdy cardstock. Little printed cards that said:

No, I'm not okay.

No, there's nothing you can do.

Then when fellow teachers asked, voices low, How are you? Anything I can do? while we grabbed notes from our mailbox cubbies, I'd hand them a card. When a new hairdresser studied my face with, Can I ask what happened to you? I see something lingering in your eyes, he'd get a card too.

Maybe I'd have another set printed with a third line:

My husband died.

Or a fourth line of fucks:

FUCK FUCK FUCK FUCK

Because sometimes I wanted to be left alone. No explanations.

And sometimes I wanted to say, Widow. Widowed. Widowhood. Show my wound: Look. Right here. See this oozing hole in my heart with its splintered glass edges. Ring-of-fire hole. See it? I know it's hard to look at. I know you wish I'd cover it up.

But it's not done burning me.

After

Feel your feelings, Emily said in an early private session while I wished for a loophole, a side door.

Even if they scare me? I asked.

Even if they do.

What I couldn't voice then was how I'd been trained to bury hard feelings. How Happy and Fine were the emotional standards, the acceptable language of drinking families. How only parents got to be angry. Then Kent died and there was no Happy. No Fine. Words for AnguishAngryHurtScaredResentmentJealousLonelyDepressedBetrayalAnxiousShameDespair were crippled even though they rippled through my gut, scorched my heart, throbbed where my hair parted.

Me hunting for a way through. The things I needed to learn.

Shame in the sediment of me. Shame Yeast from Mom who was abused as a girl, who was raised up with pinches and slaps and purple/green/yellow bruises hidden by long sleeves and dresses, who was raised up under the rule of *shush*. Her mom anger burned in words that cut and stitched in my marrow.

More Shame Yeast in the cocktail of me from Vodka Dad who was bullied by his dad. Dad who never talked about his boyhood, who drank and cheated, who abandoned our family. His anger sizzled below skin. A charcoal lava field with molten fissures. Dad who got pissed over kid things: toys sprawled in the living room, crayons and paper on the kitchen table, dirt in his car, crumbs on the couch. Even at the dusty ranch we were supposed to scrape our boots and use the boot jack to take them off before stepping in the trailer. He stopped asking, Were you raised in a barn? when I said, Kind of.

When my parents' lifepaths crossed, when Mom's Mediterranean blue and Dad's Irish emerald-green lights fused to Caribbean Sea blue, to swirls of ocean and hope like sky, they maybe voiced: We can do better. We'll have a family and raise them with love, with kindness—not with fists and belts and rage-puckered voices.

They paused their demons for a time. Stashed them in root cellars, not knowing how cool and dark breeds waiting.

They did their good enough best.

They had no tools.

Shame Yeast blooms in heat.

Guilt is feeling bad about something you did, Emily said, legs crossed, wrists crossed too. And shame? It's about feeling bad for who you are.

Shame carved a pocket deep in my left scapula, wrapped it in thorns. Shame curved my spine, my teen bones sloping into a question mark. The school nurse in eighth grade told me, You need to correct your posture. She called my mom with, Your daughter's spine is curving. It'll get worse if she doesn't do something. No, I don't recommend a back brace. Dancing can be good.

I tried dancing the curve out. All that ballet with steel-straight posture evaporated soon as I was out of pointe shoes and back in Converse tennies or my favorite cork-soled platforms. I'd leave class and go straight to slump.

I strengthened my shame muscle outside of my body too, spewed it:

Sometimes I was a mean girl to my neighbor friend when we were in junior high. One asshole time cringes me. If I didn't say it already, I'm saying it now: I'm sorry, I'm sorry.

We'd both tried out for cheerleader with a herd of girls, dreaming of pompoms and school spirit. For a week after school, I helped her learn the cheer which came easily to dancer-me. Then when we cheered in front of a committee of teachers, she made the teacher cut and I didn't.

It's not because you're good. It's because the teachers like you, I hissed at her when we plunked off the bus and started walking home.

It's because you're a teacher's pet, I said, or something like that. Then I spit poison words: You're really awful though. The kids will never vote for you.

I hope I didn't add *No one likes you* when my ugly words dumped from my mouth. That wouldn't have been true. Everyone liked her. Not being liked was my fear about me.

She half-ran to escape my meanness. Head down. Hair turning into a cape behind her even without wind. Books clamped to her chest. Jacket falling off a shoulder.

The next day her mom was at school and while I did my best to sneak by, she called me out, stared at me hard and said: Shame on you.

Fuck off—in my head, not my mouth. I knew better. I'd sulked in the principal's office before for salty language. Plus she'd tell my no-swearing mom, and while I was out of reach of spoon/spatula/hairbrush spankings, there'd be a price for my mean words: more of Mom's *you're a rotten kid* words, mashed up with the grief I felt over being a lousy kid/daughter/everything.

When Mrs. Neighbor shamed me, I remember thinking, *Shame? That's not on the menu at my house.* Except it was. While the phrase "Shame on you" wasn't served, Shame—the feeling of not enough, not good enough, not loveable, not even likeable—was a favorite dish. My wingbone twitched, the afterburn of my kid ulcer glowed, orangey-red. My body knew. I'd been shitty and I felt the burn of it.

After

I left Emily's and drove to Mom's to scoop my boy. Drove over the flat of the tide flats, thumping over railroad tracks, the arc of the curvy road to Browns Point, smells of diesel and saltwater twining. Steel clouds bullied the sky.

Rage bubbled and popped in my gut. Gurgled and spit like mini mud volcanos, thermal hot springs at Yellowstone.

How could Kent leave me?

Why did he break our life? The one that felt safe from my kid traumas and heartaches. I was finally home with him.

Abandonment lit up like sheet lightning.

I rolled down the window and screamed: Why didn't you think about our boy and me? Why'd you drive into the snowstorm when you could have turned back?

Hot face. Snotty tears sizzled on my skin.

Knot in my heart.

This mess of rage boiled in me. I didn't know how to let it move through me. I knew bury it. Tidy it up. Put a bow on it.

Later people asked why I didn't live with my parents. Even short term.

There was no moving back to where had been home.

Amy, Mom's therapist at the time, told her: Don't do too much for Annie. She doesn't want to look back and feel like you all took care of her son when she needed to take care of him.

If you're thinking, What the why? know this: My mom bravely did all the therapies when they weren't popular, when it wasn't a conversation opener: My therapist says ...

Mom started therapy in the early '50s. Early married. Wanting to carve a different path than the one she'd been raised on/raised up/dropped down.

Don't tell anyone, her mom cautioned. Please.

People will think you're crazy, her family said.

You're doing what? Dad's family said as they looked away and poured themselves another vodka or whiskey or Budweiser.

Well, Dad's mom said, making well a two syllable word, petting her church-length pearls. No one in my family needs therapy, she claimed even though Dad's dad ate pies with a fork and called his grandchildren goddamn kids, in between driving us to town from the ranch and downing shots in the bar while we kids kicked and poked each other in his Lincoln or the bed of a pickup. Even though her sons were expert drinkers.

Mom was brave. She did traditional therapy with a Freudian therapist, then with a not-Freudian therapist. She did Transcendental Meditation therapy. She was Rolfed and I worried over those bruises peeking out under long sleeves when she'd move a certain way.

Because. She wouldn't/couldn't tell us. She took Epsom salt baths, and Jan and I would hear her groan as she'd lower her body into salty hot water.

Who's hurting you? I asked and I could feel my fists clench.

No one, she said. Not J., she added because maybe she knew I was worried it was my stepdad even though that felt impossible.

Who?

It's a therapy, she said.

Therapy where they bruise you? Can I see your legs?

No.

Your back?

No.

My gut knew. She was blue purple all over.

I bruise easy, she said.

Her girl-pain carried in her body that she wanted to excavate.

Her girl-hurts bloomed through bruises: her mom hitting and pinching her little body. Making bruises where clothes hid the abuse. Her mom threatened to burn my girl-mom when she caught her looking at her own vagina in a mirror. You do that again, her mom said and struck a match. And this—she held the lit match up—goes there. She pointed to the soft between Mom's girl-legs.

I wanted to barf when Mom told me that I'll Burn Your Vagina memory. She only said it once, and later I wondered if I made it up. Grandma Sally was tender with me. I never feared her hands that yanked weeds out to their roots in one pull and opened pickle jars the first try. My grandma who lay bare legged in the grass with me and named favorite cloud shapes: angels, dragons, hearts, skulls, horses, whales. Who taught me Greek words. Who smelled like garlic and tasted like feta. Who heard garden fairies too and encouraged me to giggle and whisper with those tiny shiny somersaulting lights I saw. She cooked lemon rice chicken soup and egg custard when I was sick. She made the best meatballs. She loved me deep and wide. I've said it for years: I was her apology to my mom.

When my mom was going to the Rolfer twice a week, then once a week, and her arm bruises peaked out, leaking like a wet watercolor, she'd yank her sleeve down when she saw me looking. Part of me, even as a teenager, knew my mom was desperate to heal. And yet what mattered then were her bruises. The purple turned green turned yellow of her.

But Mom, I started when she said No to showing me her skin.

I'm not talking about it, she said and turned her bruised back, cloaked by a faded denim shirt.

She didn't trust her own voice, her own instincts. She trusted her string of therapists. So when Therapist Amy said not to do too much for me, Mom listened even though it hurt her heart.

After

That first winter with a dead husband and fish boy floating and kick-turning in his water world, I autopiloted back to teaching English 101 and 102 at Bellevue Community College. I followed the class syllabus I didn't remember creating. I read papers, scribbled grades—no comments. I gave the same writing assignment twice, and only noticed when one of my students turned in the exact same paper two times.

Was teaching two weeks after Kent died a good idea? Nah.

I didn't know what to do with my hollow heart swaddled in cobwebs. I didn't know what to do with my body that felt skinless. All insides on the outside, walking around like drawings in *Gray's Anatomy* that detail muscles and organs, that detail bones. I wanted to stay rooted to my wingback chair, staring out my living room window, crying ocean tears until it was my fish boy's swim-into-the-world time.

But I did the American thing: go back to work.

It'll get your mind off your troubles, Dad said. Dad. The compartmentalizer.

It'll give you something else to focus on while you keep growing your baby, Mom said. I don't know if it's right and I don't know what right is, she said too.

I made tiny moves. Stacked one next to another and another.

Tiny: crawled from the cocoon of my waterbed, dressed in one of two maternity overalls, whichever one smelled more vinegar/less onion. Tiny: drove the Renton S curves to Bellevue in my convertible VW Bug. Tiny: gave assignments. Collected papers. Scrawled grades. Returned papers—tear-warped, maybe a little cigarette ash smudged. Repeat. Repeat. Robot teacher. Cried and sobbed and wiped my puffy face. Struggled to not bawl while teaching. Shadow teacher. Used to Be Good teacher.

Those moves I shrugged off as tiny? They were sky sized. I swear I don't know how I did it.

Maybe I channeled my granddad who at age 17 landed in Seattle speaking only Greek. My granddad who crossed the ocean without family, who packed his smarts and his grit. My granddad who learned English, married and had a family, became a citizen (that test is hard, hard, hard), built and owned restaurants. He grinned like a wizard, stomped grapes into wine, played the piano like a piano bar man, taught us line dancing and always led. This man of fierce and kind.

I was my granddad's granddaughter. Endurance built.

I was my dad's daughter. Dad who said: I don't know can't. Dad who said: Always look forward. There's nothing to see in the rear view.

Ancestral bootstraps. My own bootstraps carved from shadows and sunlight. I pictured my kid Justin Rough Rider cowboy boots I wore in bigger and bigger sizes. How I'd yank them on and stand a little taller.

I'd slither into class—bloated with crying and no sleep and galaxies of grief. I wanted to tell students: Go do something fun, something outrageous. Climb a mountain, put your toes in the ocean or your whole body, make art, dance and sing full volume. Fuck on repeat. Do what makes you feel alive. If that's drinking or smoking pot, do that too. Don't waste your time with me. If this were your last day, you wouldn't want to spend it here.

Don't tell them that, my sister Lisa begged, her acorn-colored eyes on me, when I confessed what was hard not to say.

Why not?

What if they want to get an education? What if they live a long life and this is their launch?

I'm a terrible teacher. They should all get refunds.

You're still good, Lisa said in her good sister way.

Not.

You are. Just don't tell them nutty shit.

M&M? she asked, passing me a bag as we burrowed deeper into the russet and moss-green plaid couch, as we watched another *Bewitched* rerun and wished we had Samantha's twitchy-nose witch powers.

After

My body is too small to hold this grief.

Can I fold some in my pockets? In your pockets? Sprinkle it on love lasagna people brought in all those Pyrex dishes toppling in my freezer? Can I flavor Mom's lentil soup with tears or will it be over-salted? Can I press grief between book pages? Overfill my bookshelves? Can I hide some under composting leaves? Tuck grief in shells that hold ocean sound? In heart-shaped rocks that circle lamp bases, dot my desk, my dresser, line a garden path? Can I drop some in the tear-splashed pages I scribble endlessly, making and unmaking myself? Will grief ferment in the closet? Can I tuck some in the folds of Kent's shirts I cocoon my too-small/big body in? Or in the pockets? If I wear his shoes, will grief curl in the gap between my feet and the reach of his? If I wear his JCPenney khaki shirt, his motorcycle jacket, his cap, if I drink chamomile from his favorite tea mug, the one thrown by a potter friend? If I read more *Surely You're Joking, Mr. Feynman!*, can I be him for a hiccup of time?

See what he's seeing? Float in the stars? In the cosmos, where the size of me, the size of grief, doesn't matter?

Can I set grief down so I can breathe?

Will you hold it for me? For an hour? For two-dozen heart-beats?

Will you hold it? Catch my tears in a tear catcher? A tiny vial with a stopper to hold salty tears. Some believe grief tears are holy: that we're our most authentic self, close to spirit, as we grieve. When we're armorless. Raw. When we cry the purest tears.

I know my grief is not yours. It will boomerang back, bind the fractals of me, numb my skin, mold my spine into a question mark.

My body is too small.

No vacations. No breaks. Beats about 72 times per minute, about two-and-a-half billion times in an average 66-year life. When it's had enough, you're left for dead. Gutted. Shriveled. Heartless.

I used to lie on Kent's chest and listen to his bass-beat heart. His oceanic heart beat for 36 years. About one billion beats. I'd count. Up to 100. More. Some nights he'd read to me and I'd count those beats in time to his words, his silky voice with an allergy echo, his breath a little night sour. He almost finished "Surely, You're Joking Mr. Feynman!."

I'd add up his heartbeats, thinking: This heart. It beats him. It holds him. It beats for him and me and this other thing: the couple. It had a big job.

After

Northwest cloud day puckered with cauliflower-shaped clouds that looked like they'd been heaped in the blue. Fat clouds that rearranged the sky, blotting the golden sun and hiding Mount Rainier's saddle top. This view I counted on almost as much as I counted on suns and moons.

I locked my Ford Ranger pickup, breathed in some cloud, and joined the widows' group. Me in awe at how Liz, Maddie, Sarah, and Beth talked big things. Little things. How they shared like friends. How conversations were deep and wide. They always made room for me and sometimes I spoke in between staring at my hairy knees.

We're always going to be a group, right? Maddie said. We'll still be together when we wear shawls and use canes, right? She pushed a curly curl out of her eyes and it sprang right back.

I mean, I love my family and friends, she said, pushing that curl again. But there are widow things you all understand that they, well, they just don't.

Our heads in a sea of up and down, bobbing like kelp in the ocean, dipping under, popping up, getting tossed by waves, drifting, floating.

True, Beth said. And still … The person I most need to talk with about anything and everything is dead, she said, blowing out a big breath, motorboating her lips. It's messed up, right? I want to talk with him about my grief too, she added. But if he were here, I wouldn't need to.

I felt that too. Gratitude for these women, gratitude for my family's bottomless love, right next to my longing for Kent. Grateful for this circle and a disbelief that I needed them. Widowed at 28 still felt impossible some days. So I listened. Hard.

They talked about their triggers, where PTSD flared: ambulances, emergency rooms, sirens, construction sites. How their bodies tripped to panic, how breathing hurt, hearts pricked from walk to trot to gallop, palms itched and feet twitched. I wanted to add to their list of triggers—snow, driving in snow, plain old driving—but my words clamped tight as I bit the inside of my cheek.

I know I don't talk much here, I started and gulped an extra breath, breathing deep into an anxiety bubble in my ribs. But my words are starting to come back, I said. Before Jake was born I barely spoke. I just. Couldn't.

When Liz said she also couldn't talk in her early days, did my eyes pop? Probably. While I couldn't imagine surviving grief much less growing through it, one smidge of hope was Liz saying she didn't talk at first. Or eat. Except Xanax and Pepto Bismol. Or sleep. Maybe I was more like these women than I thought. Maybe I could grow to be more like them.

Or maybe I couldn't.

Anything and nothing at all felt possible.

After

can't imagine, people said.
Can't imagine how you feel.
Can't imagine how you're managing.
Can't imagine how you're breathing.
You don't want to, I'd say.
You don't want to.
Later I said, Go ahead and imagine.
Later I said, it feels like this:

Before

I'm tired of going so slow, Connie, another hiker, said. She flipped her straw-colored, grey-streaked braid over her shoulder.

The campfire glowed orange red. Smoke spiraled in drifts. Fifteen students and three instructors on rocks and hard ground and a downed tree. Wrapped in woods dark except the places the firelight hit. Skin. Faces. Hands.

You're only as fast as your slowest hiker, Gage, the lead instructor, said and moved a long blade of grass from one side of his mouth to the other. Pushed his Indiana Jones style hat up in front and then back down. Like a period. And this is the way it is. Code of the Woods.

Can't she go faster? one of the muscle boys asked. Or home?

Tears trickled and burned my cheeks. I was doing my best and here's the truth; I held the group up. Slowest. Weakest. Still puking from the altitude. Shouldn't be here.

Ooof, Gage said. We're all in this together for another 27 days.

After

ill I ever feel okay again? I asked on a Tuesday at group time.

Just okay. Not joy. Not bliss. Not happy. Okay felt hard enough to voice.

'Cause I still feel like I'm losing my mind some days, I said, rubbing my empty ring finger with its missing ring groove.

I'd love some okayness.

Maddie massaged her crooked pointer finger that arthritis continued to warp. Liz sighed. Big. A stuck air valve unsticking. Then.

Probably, Liz said, and smiled a fraction of a smile—almost a lip curl. She fingered her hoop earring. She eyed Emily with, Remember when I'd asked you to tell me the day I'd feel better? *Tell me the day, even if it's far from now*, I'd say. I knew I could get through anything if I had a date. Remember?

Emily smiled, her mouth wide as the sky. She cleared her throat. Her satiny salty voice: Of course I remember.

You told me you couldn't give me a date or a time. That it happens in my own time.

I asked her too! more voices said. This chorus of little animal noises—uh-huhs from us all.

Emily smiled her tender smile at each of us. This circle of love she wrapped us in every time.

How'd you get to feeling okay? I asked. Maybe that's a better question.

I felt galaxies from glimpsing okayness. And beauty on the other side? Nah. That felt impossible.

I don't think I'll ever be anything but hurt and scared, I said, and my voice warbled.

This wave of shame sloshed in my gut. Because in my girl training, as the middle daughter of a Fucked-Up Family, I'd been taught everything was shinier on a silver platter. I'd been taught to say *I'm fine* over *I'm hurting*.

And here I was: hurt and scared. And saying it out loud.

Here's something I don't want to tell you, and it kinda makes me itch in the crooks of my elbows to write it: Hard feelings undid me. Sure, I could name what happened in girlhood—raised up/ plopped down by a dad whose morning coffee was half coffee, half vodka, and a mom who built forts out of self-help books that didn't help, who denied her depression even though it coiled her and oiled my sisters and me. Me, rooted at odd angles. Layered with their poison-spewing divorce in the mid '60s. Sisters and I didn't get the We're Getting Divorced and We Still Love You Girls talk. Parents didn't know how. Dad left and drank. Mom cried lakes of tears. Sisters and I were left wondering if we were the cake or the rain in Richard Harrison's song "MacArthur Park" that Mom played on repeat, wearing a cavern in the vinyl. Seven-year-old me knew all the words. I still do.

How? I asked again to these women who I'd switched from sitting back and judging, to trusting, to hoping there was hope. I listened like my whole body was an ear.

You gotta go through it, Liz said.

There's no going around, Sarah said, her mouth in a straight line.

Keep moving through it, Maddie added. Beth nodded along with all their words, her blondness bobbing like the bouncing ball on sing-a-long lyrics.

Always remember you've got us and we've got you, they said too.

I've got no tools, I said. My stomach shriveled.

I didn't know how to say it other than to say it.

No map. No compass. No guide. Just me holding my charred heart in an offering: Here's my beaten/beating heart.

Me in slump. Grief. A concrete coat.

And while I said the tools thing, a quiet thrumming in my heart picked up its beating. Like no tools was true and not true.

Before

Today you'll learn self-arrest, Instructor Gage said and pinched the brim of his dirt-colored Fedora, this gesture where he paused, full stop, like terminal punctuation.

Who's done it before? he asked. Twelve hands to the sky. Three of us not raising hands. Especially me with my heart stampeding, throat cramping.

Fifteen students and three instructors on an ice field in the Wyoming mountains. Icy and steep and cold. Wyoming blue sky with a sunflower sun. Dressed in rain gear, not ski gear. And wool gloves that I'd soon shove in a pocket since they'd get wet, and wool wet hands are colder than bare hands. All of us gripped our ice axes: an almost T-shaped tool that so far I'd only used as a short walking stick on steep slopes. This tool with pick and shaft and head. The head of the axe was hoe-shaped on one end with a spike on the other.

Your ice axe can save your life, Instructor Kyle said when we were still in town at the NOLS headquarters the first day, gearing up for a month in the wilderness.

Remember: Mother Nature doesn't care, he said too. You gotta take care of yourself.

Mother Nature doesn't care. I'd come to think of that as a chorus along with:

1. You're only as fast as your slowest hiker.
2. It's better to slow down and keep going than to stop.
3. Carry your own weight.
4. Always take care of your feet.
5. The way through is forward.

While I'd learned how to heft my 60-pound pack up on my thigh, pass one arm through an arm strap, hop the pack on my back and cinch down the hip belt, while I'd learned how to walk—almost hike—with my monster pack, I hadn't learned to use my ice axe.

Today was the day.

Some of you will think self-arrest is fun and some of you won't, Gage said with a nod and a tug at his wooly beard. And you'll all be right.

Did he look my way when he said some of you won't? In my first 10 days of the mountaineering course, I'd shown my shitty backpacking skills. My pack knocked me over. Bruised my hips. My feet blistered and popped. I was the slowest. I swore the loudest. I cried the most and puked the hardest (altitude sickness is a bitch).

Still. This is what I wanted.

Besides. There was no side door. No fairy dust or magic wand. No shiny red Dorothy shoes to click and wish myself home. And even if I sucked at hiking and climbing (and I did), there was no giving up. I came to remagnetize myself. To let the woods rearrange me.

Watch Kyle, Gage said. He'll slide on his ass about halfway down the ice field. Then he'll flip onto his stomach with his axe angled across his chest, one hand on the shaft, one on the head. He'll dig the spiky pick in and get his weight over the axe. Up on his toes. It's almost a push-up position.

Like this.

And Gage flopped on the snow, ice axe chest high, body like a surfboard, only axe and toes in the snow. A three-pointed stance: axe and two feet gouged the ice field.

You want to turn your body into an anchor, he said.

And stop as soon as you can once you flip to your stomach. The longer it takes, the farther you'll fall. Got it?

I stared down the ice field. Steep as an intermediate ski slope. Not straight down like a black diamond slope, rated for experts. Not gentle like a beginner slope. In the middle and layered in ice.

Kyle plopped down in a sitting position and started to slide. Axe up. Feet up. No brake. He whooped and hollered as he zoomed on his ass, feet first. He carved a trail that barely dented the snow, so I knew it was mostly ice. About halfway down he flipped on his stomach, feet first, head uphill, and dug in the pick end of his ice axe. He pulled all his weight up and over the axe. Three-point stance. He maybe slid 10 feet, maybe more as he landed in halt.

You'll start to self-arrest about halfway down, Gage said. In case it takes you some real estate to stop. And see those big ol' rocks at the bottom? Gage asked and pointed at the waist-high boulders hemming the ice field.

Stop before you hit 'em. They'll mess you up.

The pulsing in my ears sped up.

Mountain cool air. Sticky palms.

Fear filled all my pockets.

Who's going? Gage half-shouted.

Me! Me! Me! yelled the muscle boys. One by one they flung their bodies down the snowy/icy slope, screaming with joy. They slid 100 feet, more. Bodies zipped down the side of the mountain until Kyle yelled Arrest! and Now! and Go! Whatever words he shouted to say it's time to flip and stop your slide. It's time to arrest yourself. They flipped. Dug axes in. They sprayed snow. They skidded to Stop.

Again! each one yelled from the bottom. Can I go again?

When there was no one left to hide behind, I swallowed extra hard.

You ready? Gage asked.

Pretend you're skiing, I told my galloping heart. *You can do this.* Surrre.

As soon as you flip onto your belly, he said, dig in your axe and get your weight over it, okay? Go at it hard. If you hold back, you'll keep sliding. You got this.

Even in long underwear, I got full-body chills.

It felt like the first time I stared down an expert black diamond slope when fear filled my body when I swallowed hard and pointed my skis down the sharp pitch when I let my skis run.

Just go, I whispered so no one could hear. Now.

I plopped on my ass and lifted my feet. Down down down. This crooked no brakes skid. Me zooming and bumping down the face of the mountain.

Now! Kyle yelled like he'd yelled for the rest of us. Flip now! And I did.

I rolled to my belly. Dug the pick of my axe into snow and ice. Dug it hard. Hard. And I kept going. Not stopping. My axe too close to my face (not my chest) as snow and ice sprayed, carving a body path.

Dig! Kyle yelled.

Dig! everyone shouted as I felt those monster boulders grow closer and bigger.

Diiig! Kyle yelled louder.

My axe chunked through the top layer of ice, making scratching sounds as I didn't stop. It felt like a fall in a dream where you know the bottom is there and you don't know it's there.

Shit! I screamed from deep in the well of me. A buzz of adrenaline. I yanked myself up over the axe, like those dreaded pull-ups in junior high gym class. Weight over the axe. Toes dug in. Body like a plank. I skidded another 10, 15, 20 feet.

Then I stopped.

I actually stopped.

No death by boulders.

No poking myself in the eye with my axe.

When I stood up and my legs shook so hard I was sure the birds could see them, Kyle yelled, Again! Now go do it again!

After five, six times zooming down the slope, ass first, belly second, self-arresting, digging toes in, toes in the mountain, a toe hold, to slow the slide, to stop, pick end jammed in ice, three-point stance, frozen fingers gripping the axe, face wet, chin scraped and bleeding.

You got it, Gage said and grinned.

If you ever fall, that's what you do, he said.

That's how you save yourself, he said, his lizard-green eyes lasered on me.

You can always save yourself. There's no mountain too big. Not a one.

After

In the deep forest where the canopy blankets the sky, where up yields more tree trunk more branches more pine needles more pinecones. Cool on my skin. Quiet under my feet. Am I barefoot? Are the needles so thick they hush my steps?

My dream space so real, I taste the evergreens.

Sun slices branches fat with bushy needles. A sliver of spotlight. There.

On the lowest branch of the nearest tree.

I've been waiting for you, Kent says, legs dangling from the tree branch in a slow swing. He grins his crooked-tooth grin. Eyes lit like a Colorado sky.

Look at this, he says, and stretches his arms wide.

Look.

He tents his brows then drops the right one.

Love bands my heart. Taut. This push and pull of love. Love swells in me wide as a river. Longing too.

Come down, I say. Will you come down?

I know I'm dreaming so I'm sure I can conjure wings. Fly to him. Or spikes on my feet so I can climb.

Look, is all he says.

Arms stretch wide. Electricity arcs out of his fingertips. Out of his crown. Currents of energy. He's his own science fair display. Perching in a tree. Glowing at the center of crackling blue light.

You see it? he asks and smiles so wide currents zip out the corners of his mouth.

Remember how you used to tell me you played with energy in your hands when you were a girl? he asks.

Chest tight. Ping on my ribs. Chest swells. Presses against the love bands.

Was it like this? he asks and moves his palms in and out, the light telescoping, contracting. I stare as the bundle of light between his hands shrinks to tennis ball size, surges to the size of a bicycle wheel. Then he switches his palms to sky and electricity arcs from his left hand to his right, his right to his left.

A trickle of tears like melting snow rivulets down my cheeks.

I'm sorry I couldn't see it when I was alive, he says.

I always loved that you could, he says. Did I tell you that?

I lift my hands. Shape them like I'm holding a playground ball. A red one. I squint, hard. Stare at the space between my hands where I used to see light play when I was a girl. Where it squeezed tiny and then bloomed as I moved my hands in and out. Where it flipped to arc, to rainbow if I turned my palms to the sky.

Eyes scrunch closed. Nose wrinkles. I peek at my bare hands. At the space between. The middle of the middle where I see straight through. No glowing light. No beams. Just unseeable air cupped in my hands. I long to see that shimmer again. My childhood companion. A comfort in my little hands.

Look, Kent says again even though I've been watching the whole time. I don't need a telescope, he says. All the stars are right here.

He waves his arms over his head. Draws air swirls around his crown. This slow dance of arms swaying around him, in rhythm. A beat. A beat I feel and don't hear. This thrumming. Pulsing. Beat of life. Prana. Chi. Holy spirit. This life force all around. He circles his hands. Wraps himself in a bubble of electricity. Tiny explosions of light. White white. White blue. Mini lightning. No thunder. He's inside the current, the storm. Where I can't touch him.

When I woke, when morning sun crept through the gaps in the blinds, when dreams were warm on my skin, I thought of girl-me playing with light.

Glitter light cradled in my girl hands, billowing in and out like I was playing Mama's concertina. The light-ball shrank and grew from watermelon to cantaloupe to plum and back. Light arced between my palms, sizzling with fuzzy edges. Light-bulb white. Blue white. Rainbow white. Shimmered between my fingers too when I spread them wide, when I squinted at the in-between space where light webs like glass fibers tickled my skin.

I didn't know everyone didn't see it until one kindergarten day when I was home from school, in a flannel nightgown with the hem frayed from worrying it, flopped on the nubby couch, orange juice and a thermometer on the coffee table, Mama in black slacks and a pressed white blouse halfway up a metal ladder, washing the taller-than-her living room windows. The smell of vinegar tickled my nose. The squeak of crumpled newspaper as she dried the glass, her arm swinging in rainbows. The madrone tree out the windows with its peely bark and soft underside, with its burnt-orange berries the birds would eat then crash into the picture windows, drunk on berries.

Look Mama, I said and held my hands out, palms up, the light between them electric.

What? she said, pushing her wavy black bangs with the heel of her hand.

See? I tried again and raised my hands, that rainbow lifting with me.

See what? She scrunched her brow—her worry look. She peeled off lemon-yellow rubber gloves and climbed down the ladder that dug its feet deeper into the goldenrod carpet.

Let me take your temperature, she said.

After

Y ou're a photograph—with your graphite hair and dark beard with flecks of nutmeg, your face in three-quarters, you not looking straight at the camera, your turquoise eyes not dots of light. Fingers curl, semi-cupping your chin. Holding yourself. This color picture with its shadow background. Almost black and white. A little grainy. Did a girlfriend before me, a photographer—lucky me—use a filter? Or is it that I've copied this picture so many times?

You're a photograph. Slick and flat. I trace your hair, your cheeks, your piano-playing fingers (you never played a piano) that curve under your chin. Thinking you. The braille of you. My fingertips remember each curve. Each texture. Satin hair. Beard like a German Shepherd's coat. Your shaved skin just above your beard line you shaved every other day. On no-shave days the prickle like an emery board, as though I could file my edges.

You have the bluest eyes, I said. I wanted to say it the moment we met, the moment your summer-sky eyes saw me. But I waited until the second time. Or was it the third?

Oh, all the little old ladies on the bus say that, you said and we both laughed. Because—that twitch in my belly—I knew it was true. You'd heard it your whole life. The bluest eyes. I wanted to say something different so I named blues: periwinkle, cornflower, Colorado sky, true.

True blue, I said, and you grinned so wide your dimple and cleft chin burrowed deeper.

You're a photograph. Trapped behind glass. No skin, no breath smells. No Irish Spring, Old Spice, deep woods, night sky smells.

My cells remember.

Can I conjure you?

Atoms once packed in six feet tall. In 200 pounds. In bass voice, belly laugh, bear sneeze. Now scattered in stardust, playing hide-and-seek in the bob of kelp beds, in the silver glint of sun on water. You are rainbows and starlight. You are my beating heart.

I dream you with all my magical thinking: wishing on stars, on moons, on oceans. Rubbing Buddha bellies, rabbit feet, four leaf clovers. I dream you on the altar at my writing desk with your kid ID bracelet, your mini Norton motorcycle, your cut and polished geode with its white swirls at the core and Lake Placid blue borders.

Our son watched Back to the Future on loop. He loved the protagonist, Marty. He played the guitar like Marty at the "Under the Sea" high school dance, scooting on his back across the hardwood floor, kicking a pretend amplifier. Of course he did.

His own kind of conjuring. All he needed was a time machine to go warn you: Go home. Don't ski. Stay with me and Mama.

You're a photograph. You used to be a poem. With the night sky in your eyes. With a timeless love that wrapped my heart, that beat out past the Milky Way, that brought me our son. The poem of you. Tattooed on my bones.

Before

Oh shit. My heart punched my chest strap, pounded in *Oh Please Oh Please is there another way?* A boulder field stretched bigger than a pasture at the ranch. With boulders double, triple my height. A massive river of rocks like giants' playthings.

I gulped. Hard. Swatted a mosquito on my arm before it could bite and add to the starry night skyscape of my skin. The constellations that had bloomed in the woods.

Swing your legs, coached Connie, whose legs stretched to my waist.

Like pendulums, she shouted.

Yeah. That'll help.

I was five foot, two inches. One hundred and forty pounds. With a 60-pound pack.

Let's go! shouted Colin, one of the muscle boys. He bounced on his toes, even in hiking boots.

Connie and Harry and Colin launched to their first rock. Then their next. They leaped from rock top to rock top. Crown to crown. With whoops and laughs and even shrieks!

Connie with her long hairy muscle legs soared boulder to boulder with a high jumper's ease. Her waist-length ponytail braid, coarse with strands of silver, floated with her.

Harry, the closest one to me and a good 50 feet away, turned back.

You got this, he yelled and stretched his hand, his kindness, to me.

Follow me, he shouted.

Fear leaked through my body like spilled used motor oil, dark and shimmery. Fear grew tentacles.

I squinted at the sun in all its bright. Cheesecloth clouds. Endless blue sky. Blue of hope. Blue of yes.

I squinted at Harry. He was grungy like the rest of us from deep woods hiking and sweating, no shower for two weeks and with two more to go. Harry with his scruffy beard and mustache waterfalling his lip. Harry with dark hair under his red felt hat and seafoam-green eyes like marbles. Harry with his hand stretched to me.

I pictured the feather I'd found and added to my pack. If I could have stroked this talisman, I would have. Instead, I hooked my thumbs at the shoulder straps and crouched slightly in that athletic I'm Ready way. Then, with my arms out to my sides, I launched from my safe rock to the massive one in front of me. I stuck it. Sort of. I wobbled as my pack slammed into me, pushing me forward, down. Still, I stuck.

Again! Harry shouted, and I knew he was right. Keep moving. Keep jumping. Keep picking my way through the boulders one leap at a time.

Falling down didn't matter.

Getting up did.

Harry pointed to a flattish topped rock in: Go there next. I followed his pointing for a leap or two or ten. Then waved him on.

I needed to carve my own path.

For an hour, more, I jumped, crawled, clawed my way from one boulder to the next. I landed on feet and knees and ass. My knees bled. My shins too. My breath sounded like a backhoe digging gravel. New bruises would sprout from smacking body parts to rocks.

The next gap yawned wide. But climbing down and back up was slow and already I'd lost sight of Harry and way lost sight of Colin and Connie.

Just jump.

What's the worst that can happen?

I sucked air deep in my belly. A Buddha breath. A Let's Go breath.

I took one step back for extra power and I leaped. Boulder to boulder. Gap to gap.

My Frankenstein boots with almost no bend in the soles pounded the boulder. But not the top. I smacked the granite a few feet below its crown and curled my toes uselessly. My fingers clawed against the bumpy rock, searching, but there were no cracks.

I slid straight down. Crash landed on my back with thud. Stuck in the crack between boulders. My pack wedged in tight with the weight of me.

I yanked my shoulder straps.

Nothing.

I wiggled to sit up. Wiggled to roll sideways.

Nope.

I kicked the rock. Hard. To pry my pack a sliver toward free.
Nothing.

Motherfucker! I yelled and strained for an echo.

Nope.

Did you hear me? I screamed to the blue, blue sky.

Motherfucker!

Then I saw myself. This little human in a giant boulder field.
On her back like the proverbial bug. Flailing arms and legs. Stuck.
Stuck. Stuck. I was Gregor Samsa in Kafka's *The Metamorphosis*,
who wakes up as an insect, a "Venus in Furs." I was every little
bug I found as a girl when their little legs wiggled and I'd flip
them over.

And then.

I started to laugh. First a snort-laugh that lit a laugh bubble
in my root, at the tip of my tailbone. A bubble that grew and
bloomed more bubbles as it spindled up my spine, spilled into
my gut, flooded the pockets of my core, my body, my being. My
laugh cracked the boulders and mountains and sky.

My laugh cracked me open.

I was laughing and crying and oh gawd I needed to pee.

After

I dream about Kent packing my backpack.
He rerolls my clothes. Stuffs air pockets with socks.
You'll want your glacier goggles. Not these wimpy sunglasses,
he says, resting my Ray Bans on the nightstand.
I like those sunglasses, I say, my voice with a hiccup.
You'll have to carry all the water. And the purifying tablets.
Don't forget them, he adds as he waves them over his head and
then tucks them in a pocket of my pack.
Remember your map.
And compass.
I know how you get turned around. Worry inks his words.
I'm not ready, I say. I need you.
You'll be fine.
I showed you what I could.
I left you with our boy.
Now you'll show him.

Come with me, I beg. One more time. One more hike. One more snow cave. One more laugh. Dance. Talk. One more baby. One more anything. Please.

And remember the essentials, he says. Carry them all.

Five more minutes? I ask.

I filled your water bottles.

I stare at all the water—the heaviest essential.

Remember, he repeats like maybe I'm not listening (I'm not). Remember the essentials. All 10 of them.

Love. Grace. Kindness. Gratitude. Generosity. Acceptance. Forgiveness. Integrity. More love. Skies of love.

What if the heart had a fifth chamber? Or more? What would be stored? More love? Hurt? More of what makes us, us? People say eyes are the windows to the soul. Okay. But what about the heart? The seat of the soul. I love you with all my heart, we say. I love you with all my stretched, moved, touched, battered, broken, mended, healed, swollen, drenched in honey heart.

After

A Field Guide to Christmas Grief

1. Ask your mom and sisters to check on you daily like you haven't for a while. That need has swam back to you in your fears around navigating this first Christmas as a widow. Ask them to call because picking up the phone hurts even though you want to hear their voices. Because they're shiny life rafts in your ocean of lonely. Later this is something you'll do for others because it meant everything to have it done for you.

2. Once you've tended to your heart, consider some do-ing-ness that can get you through December. Just consider.

3. Buy a fire-engine red sweatshirt with Bah Hum Bug in big block letters and lights twining through the Bah and the Hum and the Bug.

4. Ask the salesperson if the sweatshirt comes in black or if there's one that says Merry Fucking Christmas. When she says No with a wince, go ahead and buy the red Bah Hum Bug one.

5. Wear the sweatshirt every day. Every. December. Day.
6. Wash it when it stinks. Do this at night so you can wear it the next morning.
7. Leave Christmas decorations in the spare-room closet, in their boxes. Yes. Even the stocking your mom knit when you were a girl, knit with your name on top and Santa's beard in angora. Knit with love. Even though you've hung it every Christmas.
8. No Christmas lights. You can tell the story of ten-year-old you and your stepdad making a giant star in the naked maple tree, star so big you needed an extension ladder to string the lights. You'll always have that story.
9. Do not bake Christmas cookies. When I say cookie, I mean no spritz, sugar, shortbread. Nothing to decorate with icing. No lemon bars or chocolate crinkles. No biscotti.
10. Do not bake no-bake cookies.
11. Forget Christmas cards—they're a bitch even in a good year.
12. Zero Christmas carols, not on the stereo, in the car. Oh, avoid stores that play "Holly Jolly Christmas" endlessly. Unless carols bring you comfort. Unless Doctor Demento carols still make you laugh.
13. Gift buying? Nah … wait. Give everyone a picture of Jake. Hand them out. Don't wrap them the way Mom taught you to make beautiful packages. All those handmade bows. Skills you can use later if you choose.
14. If you must watch a Christmas movie, make it the English version of *A Christmas Carol*, all black and white and grainy and crackly, all Jacob Marley clanking his forever

chains, his pain he's doomed to carry, his pain he longs to help his friend avoid.

15. Stare out the kitchen window. Ash-colored sky. Clouds plump with rain. Stare and remember a year ago when you were pregnant and bursting bubbles of Christmas joy. When you wore Kent's Icelandic sweater daily because it fit and you loved its cozy. When you dreamed of this year and your boy's first Christmas, how your family of three would pack it in bliss.

16. Cry.

17. Cry monsoon tears.

18. Cry avalanche tears.

19. Wipe your snotty face with the hem of your Bah Hum Bug sweatshirt.

20. Breathe. Breathe some more.

21. Consider how to make art with grief.

22. Paint your own tree. A blue tree on oversized poster board.

23. Look up the Chinese hanzi for grief and do your best to copy it.

24. Ask Leo—Jake's godfather who is Chinese—if grief in Chinese means *danger and opportunity* like you've been told.

25. Half smile when Leo corrects you with *dangerous opportunity*. Westerners get so hung up on yin and yang, he adds. Not everything is yin and yang, he says with a mini eye roll.

26. Paint hanzi grief all over your blue tree, like ornaments. Black squiggles on a blue tree. A bruise of a tree. Your new Christmas memory.

27. Find 12 flattish round rocks and nestle them at the base of your blue tree. Gifts. Moons. One for each month that

you've kept yourself and your boy alive. Write words on the bottom of the rocks, where they're hidden, where they're just for you.

28. When your dad comes over and asks, Annie, where's your tree? Show him the blue with black one you made even though he won't understand.

29. When your dad comes back the next day with a mini pine tree, in a mini pot, maybe a foot tall, real and piney smelling, decorated with foil squares, like packages, the size of sugar cubes, tell him Thank you. Because you know he loves you. Because you know he's worried about you. Because he finds your blue tree disturbing.

30. When you and your dad rock on your heels at the same time, this DNA gesture, hands in pockets, him jingling loose coins like he does, you searching pocket seams for lint. When this happens? Half smile.

31. Know your dad is doing his best to let you have your grief while you are doing your best to not pretend.

32. Days when you can manage a little self-care, make your bed. Maybe wash the sheets. Use your favorite comforter and extra pillows. This comfort nest that calls like siren song. Let the warmth of your waterbed cradle you like the ocean.

33. Write in your journal. Draw too.

34. If you can peek out from under your sad and your achy heart, do something for another. Make a donation to the Rescue Mission. Because while money is thin as thin, because while you pick your cuticles to bleeding over bills, you have a home and food. Not having extra is still having plenty. Do a little good where you can.

35. Remember December 25th is a sun and moon long. December 26th is coming too. You can hold the hard next to knowing it will pass. One in each hand. You at the center. Let them talk to each other. What will they say?

36. Ignore everything on this list. Or pick some of the things. Or make a new list. Or thumb through your traditions and do any that soothe. Be kind to your tender heart. Be kind to you.

After

New Year's Eve. Good Night year. Dead husband year. New baby year. Year of mashed heart. Year of mama heart. Year of swimming on the bottom of ocean tears. Year of fire. Year of Pele: Hawaiian goddess of fire. Year of the phoenix. That fire bird, reborn from ashes image Jake will tattoo on his bicep—wings of fire in black, gold, and apple red—when he's in college.

I cradled the phone, ear to shoulder. Folded my clean Bah Hum Bug sweatshirt and tucked it in a bag to donate.

Come over, Jan said. Let's be together.

But ... I felt swamped by tired. A tired that anchored me to the couch, my wingback chair, the bed too. Winter dark amped up my stay-in-bed feeling, my oh-that-comforter-looks-nice feeling.

Do, Jan said. Together is better.

My sister's cozy one-bedroom apartment by the Puyallup River. Shag carpet, smoky mirrors with tiny veins of gold over the fire-place, popcorn ceilings. The Puyallup River flowed by the sprawling gecko-shaped apartment building. In soggy winters sometimes the river flooded and soaked the lower apartments. Warm nights Jan opened the sliding glass door. Water trickled and raced around rocks, big granite grey ones in the river and on the banks. Even with winter cold and the sliding doors closed, you could feel the river. Fingers of wet cupping rocks. Fingers of wet strumming a love song.

The mantle clock ticked. The minute hand jerked and circled the white clock face with its black roman numbers.

Almost midnight.

Here, Jan said and handed me a foil-colored noisemaker with paper fringe, a sparkly "HAPPY NEW YEAR!" hat with fringe too.

You made it, she said. Dark eyes bursting with light. Her one dimple. Black hair. Fair skin. Cherry-red lips. Snow White sister. Got-your-back sister. I'm-right-here sister.

She blew her noisemaker. Unfurled. Squeaked. You did! she cheered. And that's not nothing.

Ping in my chest. Tiny black dots floated in front of my eyes too. Some single, some double barbells. These tiny dots I've seen since I was a girl. Dots out of reach. Untouchable. Truth signals.

I plunked on the metallic, green paper hat with its thin elastic strap. Blew the noisemaker that rolled out and in. Fast. Serpent tongue. Tongue with blare and squeak and *Hey I'm here let's make some noise.*

Bye-bye, 1987! I yelled. Voice a hammer.

Thank you for Jakester! I cheered and tweeted the paper horn again.

My boy on his quilt—a handmade, lovemade one covered in planes and cars and trucks, all things going places. His hazel eyes that sometimes leaned blue, sometimes green. His long and leanish body, like he'd be his whole life. With his pea toes and grip fingers. With his chest now bigger than I could circle with my hands, like I could when he was born.

It was creeping on to midnight and he was still awake. Not a big sleeper, my boy. Those first few months neither of us slept. Most days my eyelids clicked. Some days my clothes were inside out. All days I adored him. My love bigger than the ocean.

Jake stretched long, flung his feet in the air, grabbed one foot to his mouth. Then he rolled to his stomach, propped himself up, sphinxlike, smiled and drooled. Yoga baby. Supple and tender and strong baby.

You amazing baby you, I cooed as I scooped him up, slipped a "HAPPY NEW YEAR!" hat on him and danced around the room. We did it, I sang. We're here! You're here! I love you, Jake-O!

I nuzzled his neck. Breathed in his baby powder, anything is possible smell.

That fifth chamber in my heart bumped and thumped. Swelled with love. Gratitude. Right at the intersection of the atria and ventricles. Where the hole was. Now stitched with lightning, stitched with love. The fifth chamber, bigger than a pod, not yet as big as its sister chambers.

Hello 1988! I laughed and spun around with my boy snug in my arms. This vortex of joy. Jake smiled and paddled his bare feet, gripped my shoulders with his suction-cup fingers.

What? Jan puzzled at me, her eyebrows pitched.

What?

You laughed. I heard you laugh.

I blinked and pushed my lower lip out like I do.

You did, she said, her mouth bell-shaped on *did*.

You laughed. A real laugh.

And it hit me: I hadn't laughed hard in a year. Not a true belly laugh.

Damn, I said and wiped the corners of my eyes. Laughing tears. Happy tears.

Let's do something more than tweet paper horns, I said and stood a little taller.

Okay. But what?

Outside the river rolled and bumped and wet up the rocks. The night sky, midnight blue. Blue to black. Tinsel of stars between breaths of clouds. The moon bright over the river. The moon reflected in a megaphone of light.

You have a calendar? I asked.

Sure.

Let's burn it.

Jan smiled, half-skipped out of the living room, and returned waving a Sierra Club calendar over her head like a trophy. When she ripped off the cover, it made that paper tearing rrriiippp that reminded me of last days of school and shredding spiral notebooks.

We'll get it started with this, Jan grinned, lighting the cover and tossing it in the empty fireplace with its smoky mirror and rivulets of gold.

I get January, I said, laying claim to what I knew my sister would give.

I set Jake on his quilt with its planes and trains and trucks, with his spine like rebar. He clapped his little boy clap, fingers splayed.

January, I told him, sucked.

I flicked the blue Bic lighter, placed the flame on January 13th. The paper warmed and browned and caught fire. A hole in the middle of the month, like the hole in my heart, the hole that had swallowed days forward and backward: 14, 15, 16, 17, 18, 19,

20, 21, 22, 23, 24, 25, 26, 27, 28, 29, 30, 31, 12, 11, 10, 9, 8, 7, 6, 5, 4, 3, 2, 1.

I tossed the flaming month in the fireplace mouth before it burned me.

Goodbye January.

Good-fucking-bye.

I grinned at my sis. This woman. Sister connection. Sister love. Deep and strong. This cord between us. This woman I'd loved and fought with and loved some more. Love in an infinity loop, like an 8. Sometimes tight in the center, at the cross of the *X*. Sometimes loose in the curves. Tendrilled through time.

Shit, that felt good, I said. A little sizzle-pop in my belly. A squiggle of good.

I tore off February and offered it to my sis.

February sucked too, she said. The Bic lighter on the corner of the month. February smoked and caught. Flamed yellow and orange.

I didn't know how to help you, she said. It was awful. We did our best.

We burned up 1987. Torched winter and days of me glued to my wingback chair. Its spine my spine. Winter skies. Grey like my heart. Sky tears. My tears. My family's tears. The tears of Kent's family. Oceans and skies of tears that flooded the mourners' sea.

We burned spring and memories of stomping on crocuses, hissing as trees leafed out. We burned Kent's 37th birthday, March 2nd. The first birthday he didn't have.

April was next. Jake's birthday month. Spring baby with dark eyes and flawless skin, who changed every day, who pulled me back. Back through the ether. Back through black holes and starlight and time worms. Tethered me to life and growth and hope too.

May. Mother's Day. Pajamas with tears and a pack of Marlboro Lights (less harsh than Marlboro Reds) until Jan peeled me off the couch, nudged me into jeans and a T-shirt, and drove to Mom and J.'s. Rooted on their loveseat, I stared at Puget Sound. Deep blue. Sea blue. Mermaid blue. Wooly clouds. Oyster sky.

Your first Mother's Day. Let me take your picture, Mom said then, and I waved her off.

We burned summer: saffron sun, emerald grass, sparklers, burgers on the grill, iced coffee, shorts, sunburns, ponytails, and lost sunglasses. By August we laughed more than cried. This frenzy of burning and remembering and letting go.

The fire in my sister's fireplace with the wide mouth and smoky mirrors. Fire. It was bonfires at the ranch as girls when I'd catch a stick on fire and write my name in the night sky. Sear it into the black of night. It was pounding the hot end of my stick with a rock, pretending to be a farrier, shaping horseshoes. It was beach fires in college. Me building the teepee of wood. Feeding the fire. Huddled around the blaze in swimsuits and beach towels. It was mini fires while backpacking. Rings of stones. Licks of flames. Snow camping and brandy sniffers of warm. Me cuddled up with Kent.

We laughed. Hard. Wiped our eyes and burned through fall. We laughed at the best part: Mom's Thanksgiving table. Mom's table. Normally straight out of *House Beautiful* with French linens and Spode china and silver silverware. This year the silver platter was foil. We had a Mickey Mouse tablecloth, mismatched dishes, paper cups, and red and purple candles in the tarnished candelabra.

Nothing's normal, Mom said. We might as well show it.

December. Depression's rocket fuel.

I tore December in two, careful to split December 25th, and handed Jan half.

You and your Bah Hum Bug sweatshirt, she said and laughed.

Goodbye, December! Goodbye, Christmas cheer! I shouted as I tossed my half in the fireplace.

So long, 1987! Jan sang as she tossed her flaming half of December in with mine.

We grabbed each other's wrists, leaned back and spun in circles like we did when we were girls when we laughed and spun and tried to get the other to fall first. We tossed our heads back in the spin and shouted, So long 1987! I felt like teen-me, shrieking with my sister, like when I'd drive with her at my side on the bench seat of our stepdad's Ranchero, and sometimes we'd roll the windows down and scream as loud as we could or howl like the wolf pack we've been from the start.

Jake rubbed his eyes with his tiny fists. He stared at his auntie. Then me.

I scooped my boy to my hip and held Jan tight with my other arm.

It's okay, Sweets, I cooed. This is a fine kind of crazy.

The best kind, little sis said.

The you're-going-to–be-all-right kind.

He blinked his leggy lashes—dark fringe lining his goldeny eyes that leaned blue this New Year's Eve.

I love you, Bud, I said and kissed the crown of his head.

You're the best of 1987.

The wet of the night pressed against the sliding glass doors.

A cloud blanketed the moon.

Let's do it again, I said.

And we laughed so hard I peed a dribble.

After

Do things get better after the first year? I asked my widow posse when the first anniversary of Kent's death napped in the edges, looming, along with my double-down grief body aches: headaches, heavy shoulders, heart thumping, not THUMPING. My stuffing unstuffed like the early days.

They checked the ceiling, checked their shoes for a beat.

Later they told me: Here's what people don't say. The second year becomes the first anniversary of your first-year losses. The second year you spend time remembering how you navigated the first year, thinking about how now it's your second year of missing the big dates, the small dates. They didn't say those words until I crawled through the first-year anniversary. As that mountain anniversary tracked closer, they said: We're here. We love you.

A year without the love of my life.

Are you better? people asked.

(Please tell me you're better.)

How'd you do it? people wondered.

(Please tell me in case I ever need to know.)

Are you over it? Have you healed? The questions under the questions.

No.

I don't know.

No.

Actually, fuck no.

You don't get over grief. It's not the flu. Your heart grows around your grief. Your heart fills in the cracks, those cracks that let the light shine through. You become your own kintsugi piece.

You get up. You get knocked down. In daylight. In nightlight. You think endlessly about your beloved until you realize you didn't think about them one whole day. Crap! Then you double down on remembering. You learn to lean into the people holding you up. You find new people you can circle with. You make micro moves to let the story you wanted melt to the background, living in shadow, as you wonder about the story you have, as you begin to let your new story be most alive, as you step into who you are in the After, as you realize widowed is what happened. It's not who you are.

That first anniversary?

It unstitched me. Until it didn't.

I spent it in the arms of Mom and sisters. I spent it thigh to thigh with the women who loved me best.

Jake on all our bodies. This circle of women who held him.

On the couch, in pajamas, a Kent shirt loose over my flannels, snotty Kleenex in tumbledown pyramids.

Sisters brought things Kent liked: German chocolate cake, rum balls, Cherry Coke. Of course there were M&Ms, my favorite grief food. Sweet, crunchy, smooth little pebbles, that faint clicking sound they made when I ran my hand through them. Lisa brought them in a gift bag that felt bottomless. Hello friends.

I placed Kent's running shoes by the front door where he'd left them, untied. His tea mug on the kitchen counter. I filled it with chamomile tea and let it cool. I'd recycled the last newspaper he read or I would have pulled it out too. I took some weird comfort in the details, restaging objects like they were on his last day, like I left them for months as though he'd step back into his Nikes.

I squatted next to my wingback chair to say *Hello* and *I love you* to my year-ago self. Numb me, who last year stared at one leggy cobweb and imagined herself someplace else where husbands didn't die and leave their pregnant wives. Time is artificial. I imagined reaching through the worm of time to hug 28-year-old me. To tell her it's okay to stay in her chair as long as she needs. To tell her I'm sorry I ditched her a year ago. To tell her we'll still carry the deep yearning for what was and never will be and that it's okay. It's all grief. To tuck a handkerchief in her closed hands. An embroidered one from our Greek grandma that we've had since we were a girl.

First anniversary. In wedding anniversaries the first one is yellow or gold. What's the color of a deathiversary? One year—what's the color? What's the shade? Fog. Pewter. Dove. Dove sliding to charcoal with black inked in like the end of day sky as the sky bruises up.

Day tumbled to night as it does. When I got sleepy enough and worn out from sobbing, when Jake folded into sleepy, his tiny fists unfisted, and Mom tucked him in his crib, my sisters hugged me, with We love you and Do you want us to stay?

I think I can sleep, I told them. I love you endlessly.

I scrunched down in my waterbed, pulled the comforter chin high, changed my mind, half sat-up and smoked a couple of cigarettes. I read my journal of the first year without Kent and bawled over my sad words. My ache and no hope. My bottomless bottom. Pages warped with tears and scribbles: I'm sad, broken, lonely, miserable. Ink-smeared, I don't think I can do this words. Sprinkled with I don't know how and somehow I will words. I flipped the page and wrote this:

Writing's saved me this grief year.

I scratched that out and wrote this:

I saved myself writing.

Then I wrote more:

A year ago my husband died. I was six-months pregnant with our only child. Those are two sentences I couldn't write until a few months ago. But now I can and it means, what? That I can write the worst thing that ever happened to me. And maybe if I can write those sentences, maybe I can see Kent's death for what it was: the end of his life.

It doesn't have to be the end of mine.

After

How are you today? Therapist Emily asked, as she settled into the saddle-colored leather chair that squeaked like leather does. I always loved that she added *today*, not solely the worn-out How are you? that felt too big in grief to answer.

Tuesday. Group day. Liz leaned back, tugged at the hem of her heather-grey sweatshirt, propped her right foot on her left knee, her mama heart pulsing like a beacon. A lifeline loveline that anchored me. Maddie grinned her cherub grin, scrubbed her hands together. Sarah pulled at the peplum of her fitted suit jacket and sat up a little straighter. Beth shook construction dust from her hair. Remodel's going great! she said. Thumbs up. It'd be weeks before she realized she bought a gas stove and didn't have gas in her house, or noticed she forgot to include kitchen drawers.

I felt a gush of love for them all. Widow squad. We Got You squad. Here for the Happy and Sad squad.

Good, I said to Emily's How are you today question. How weird is that? I bit my bottom lip. Breathed a jagged breath. An ocean deep in my throat.

Emily smiled her closed-lipped smile that spread across her kind face. Not weird, she assured. Her voice tender.

I kinda feel normal, I said, raising my hands in my What the what? gesture. And that's weird, I added. My throat cracked. These words, so foreign in grief time, felt right.

It's been normal to feel weird, Emily said, her coffee-bean dark eyes soft. She leaned in. And now it's weird to feel normal.

Her words were a salve. True words. Not just Here's What to Say words.

Really weird, I said. Full stop. I tucked my hands under my thighs. Rocked east to west. Felt my trotting heart playing rib scales.

And I wasn't singled out, I added, relief coloring me a rainbow of colors.

For so long I felt singled out—punished, like I deserved to be broken. My left scapula pinched, this body pinch where I carried shame. It flexed when I voiced a truth I'd buried. Because. When you're told You're fine on repeat, the truth of not-fineness burrows into your folds. When you grow up with silence and hurts, you think you deserve brokenness.

How are your girls handling everything? Mama's friend asked, her voice on low.

Seven- or eight-year-old me slammed to a stop in the hall where they couldn't see me, where I could listen.

Well, Lisa is acting out some, Mama said, and I heard her breath breathing out, the long exhale of cigarette smoke in a cone-shaped stream.

Of course, her friend said, and blew out cigarette smoke too. Salem Menthols: Mama's brand. Pretty normal, I'd think, the friend said, and I pictured them both nestling cigarettes in the pearl-white ashtray that was Mama's favorite, or maybe they were near the end of their smokes and crushed the cigarette butts.

She'll be okay, Mama quickly added, like she could make everything okay by using the okay word.

And Jan's a baby, Mama went. So, you know, she's okay.

What about Annie?

My chest turned to concrete. I pretended I was small as a squirrel.

Oh, she's fine, Mama said.

The click, snap of a lighter. The long in-breath, long out-breath. The grey smell of cigarette smoke curled down the hall toward me.

She's Annie. She's always fine.

My throat on fire. No. My throat flooded in feathers with the feathers tickling and the quill ends poking. I needed to cough, to puke. I needed to scream: I'm not fine. I'm scared and hurt and confused. Why'd Dad leave? Was it my fault? Is he coming back? What did I do to break my family?

Lisa? Annie? Mama said. Who's there?

I turned and tiptoed down the hall with its slate floor that was cold and noisy. Glad I wore socks. Soon as I passed the bathroom, with Lisa on the other side of the locked door, I sped up, got to my room, launched myself onto my bed, opened a book, and pretended I'd been reading. I made sure the book was right-side up because I was upside down. I plucked my favorite marble from the nightstand, the indigo one with lizard-green and cloud-white swirls. The one I was sure was the world. The one that soothed. I popped it in my mouth. Clicked it against my teeth. One ear listened to my squirrel heart (thump bump thump bump), one for Mama's footsteps that didn't come.

But I wasn't, I told my widow squad. Singled out, I mean. And holy everything, I sure didn't deserve Kent dying. I said those words and my body felt soft: no holding, no twitching.

My eyes swept the circle. Widow posse. While we were different in so many ways, our grief twined us. Our group a grief braid. Each widow stronger, softer, deeper, wider for the weave of the over and under and through braid. For the places the braid frayed and the places it didn't.

They nodded, yes, yes, yes.

You're going to be okay, Emily said. Do you know that?

It might not feel like it all the time, she said.

It happens in small and big ways.

Do you know you're okay?

I'm no caterpillar to butterfly, I said, a sound fluttering out of me some place between a sigh and a grunt. Not yet anyway.

Maybe I was in the chrysalis stage. That in-between where metamorphosis lives. Where caterpillars melt to goo before they stitch a new body. Not butterfly. Not shimmer turquoise wings. Wet from their cocoon. Then dry. Then fluttering and flying. Not yet.

And yeah, I'm going to be okay.

I surprised myself when that okay word slipped out. And maybe for the first time, I felt the traction of it.

After

At moments when I was undone, a shadow of myself stumbling and sobbing and desperate for a little relief, sometimes I'd feel a mini Kent cyclone. I'd feel him hugging me from behind, wrapping cool on my collarbones. A tickle on my earlobe. A non-kiss kiss. His impossible heart pressed to my spine. The stardust of him cracked through the veil, star skin to my skin.

My arm hairs would stand straight up. Tingles would splash my chest and arms. A wave would curl from my scapulae up my spine up the base of my neck up the back of my head.

I'd hear Kent whisper: I'm sorry. I'm sorry. I love you.

If I turned to see him, he'd be—snap—gone.

I learned to not turn. Stay quiet in the quiet of me. Let him be with me in the only way he could.

After

All good stories have a turning point.

The truth is, a big turn came when I bought new jeans. How could such a hard story have such a fluff turn? It did. It does.

Jake sat spine-straight in his stroller with his favorite red rings teething toy that reminded me of Saturn's ring. This one splattered with teeth dents. I strapped it to his stroller so it would stay attached when he cast it overboard, so he could reel it in under his own power.

I breathed into my belly, my feet. Three, four, five belly breaths to calm my revving nervous system. Anxiety spiked when I took myself and Jake out in public. Mostly I didn't. Or if I did, I had Mom or a sister with me.

I can do it, I'd told Mom and sisters. I gotta practice being in the world, right?

One more big breath, then a smaller breath where I told myself, I got this, before pushing us both into The Bon Marché, our local department store, with its overhead ticking fluorescent lights and fake smiling mannequins and sticky lingering perfume smells. I navigated the main floor of makeup, jewelry, accessories, more. Did my best to smile at the women who waved all four fingers at Jake in that slow wave used for babies. Finally to my goal: women's casual.

Can I help you find something? asked the salesperson with tall heels and a flat stomach, as I grabbed five, maybe six pairs of jeans in pre-baby and now-baby sizes.

I got it, I said, as I wheeled us both to the dressing room, then fished Cheerios out of a mini-Tupperware to keep Jake busy.

Jeans off. Jeans on. Off. On. My old size six—too tight. New size eight—okay.

Do you need anything? asked the salesperson while I twisted side to side—front view, profile, ass—in the dressing room's full-length mirror and smirked at my body. I poked my mashed potatoes belly. Wondered if my stomach muscles would ever be muscles again. I thought I was fat. Gawww.

I want to reach through words and time, tell younger me how beautiful she is. Every part of me, especially that soft belly that stretched and cradled my boy.

I'm okay, I said to the salesperson. My first lie that day.

Do you need a different size? she asked through the closed door, just her heels and sapling lower legs showing.

No thanks, I said, pushing words out through mouth fuzz as I poked my squishy belly.

Do I buy the bigger size and eat more M&Ms?

Nah.

I settled on the too-tight pair and slithered home. Reversed all the things I'd done to get us to the store: Jake out of his car seat, stroller in the garage, house alarm off.

We did it, Bud, I told Jake even though I was talking to myself. He cooed to my half smile and kicked his running feet. Grinned his grin. Drooled his perfect drool.

I yanked new jeans from their shopping bag. My trophy: size six Calvin Kleins like I wore before my boy.

But.

The pair I brought home? Size eight. Right there on the label. I busted into tears. No warm-up. A gush of wet.

In that moment everything hard about my life was stuffed inside those jeans. Grief filled pockets. Doubt, fear, and depression wrapped belt-buckle loops. All my I-suck-at-life stitched in the topstitching.

If I couldn't do something as simple as this, how could I do anything bigger?

I wanted to torch those size eights with dragon breath. Sizzle them to ashes. I wanted to curl up with my tears.

While my face pinked up, Jake rolled onto his belly, lifted his head and chest like a sphinx, and laughed. His baby laugh shook him toes up.

His laugh? It rolled back the dark.

You're right, I said. You brilliant baby, you.

In that moment, the always choice between tears and laughter hit me hard. It was just a pair of jeans. I mean, come on.

My boy stared his open wonder stare that mashed my heart, that said *You got this*, that said *Hey Ma, it's only jeans*. If he could have shrugged, he might have.

He rolled on his back, his front, his back, his front. He inched forward on his belly, commando style, one arm in front, the next arm in front, concentrating to snake his little body inch by inch.

This hardworking baby. If he could work so hard, I could too.

Watch me.

I refolded the jeans, tucked them in the bag, back to the Bon, back to the salesperson, back to swapping jeans for jeans. As I popped size six in the carry pocket of Jake's stroller, I felt bubbles of proud. And a joy feeling, a little sizzle pop behind ribs. It sizzled and popped. I'd done this seemingly small thing, what would have been small in my Before life, and it was super-sized. While I had more healing, I also felt the pull of *I can*. The sun on my face meeting my own sun, reminding me, happiness was my true nature, remembering *I got this.*

After

I have a friend. Wanna meet him?

Batteries or body?

Body.

No thanks.

When you're ready for fun, let me know.

Uh.

There's this guy who teaches at another college.

No thanks.

Gal?

Ha. Still no thanks.

You've worked so hard. Can you give yourself a break? Have a little fun?

Maybe.

Had I glimpsed the Maddie crossroad: single and going on a date? Could I be like Maddie and my other widow squad loves who were dating?

Maybe.

Because.

My body. Rolling over. Stretching. Cracking neck muscles. Hello body.

You've been here all this time? Been here this year and a half I've ignored you?

Yup. Snoozing in the deep freeze. Hibernating. Growing fuzz thick as rainforest moss. Libido on stall. Neurotransmitters not transmitting.

Then.

A squiggle of desire.

Libido dial spinning from whisper to shout: Hello! Over here! In the tangy of me.

Before and After

Ten Essentials
1. Navigation: map, compass.
2. Headlamp/flashlight plus extra batteries.
3. Sunglasses and sunscreen.
4. First-aid supplies.
5. Pocket knife. Leatherman.
6. Fire: waterproof matches, tinder, stove. Dryer lint in a Ziploc.
7. Shelter. Light as an emergency blanket for day trips. Tent and tarp for overnight.
8. Extra food (even though it's heavy and will come home bruised).
9. Extra water. The heaviest essential: over eight pounds per gallon heavy. Plus a way to purify it—tablets and/or pump.
10. Extra clothing: one dry layer.
11. Heart in your hand.

Before

Blisters hardened to callouses. Bruises to leather skin. The cut of muscles. Hairy calves firm like I hadn't had since ballet and pointe shoe years. Biceps too. More than I'd ever had. A steadiness in my stride. Feet firm to the ground. The ground in me. As my body morphed to beast mode, joy bubbles percolated in my chest up my throat out my crown. I didn't know in the Wyoming mountains under my beasty 60-pound pack that I was also building psyche muscles, emotional muscles, muscles to hold me up when I needed them most. All the ways I showed myself *I Can* in the woods. I'd need and use every ounce of brave I carved into myself the month I spent in the backcountry. I thought I was facing my past when I was actually facing my future.

After

efore I said Yes to meeting Scot, I stared into the dark. Talked to night shadows. Rolled rocks between fingers. Made spirals out of heart-shaped rocks. Lingered with the moon. Pulled tarot cards, burned incense, burned sage. I played the games I played as a girl—if the next thing I say is an even number of words, the answer is Yes, going. If I turn on the radio and the song is a love song, Not going. I unearthed my old Magic 8 Ball with its fuzzy answers: Without a doubt. As I see it, yes. Don't count on it. Better not tell you now.

Hoping for magic.

Hoping for signs.

Terrified of risking my heart.

Terrified of not risking. Of staying in the dark.

Before saying Yes, I asked my friend and mentor Marilyn, who knew Scot, if Scot was a Dick (her beloved husband) or a Kent and she said: How could he be? Those two are taken.

I finally turned away from fear. Or at least I side-eyed fear.

I didn't know if my black leather skirt would fit after having Jake, after my runner's body softened to a mama body even though I'd reclaimed running. Even though I only gained 20 pounds with my boy because—um—because I mostly stopped eating after Kent died. The day Jake was born I could zip my parka over my belly.

You can't have that baby yet, someone said the week before Jake made his splash in the world. You're too small.

Watch me.

Stop at Frisko Freeze, my obstetrician told me every visit those last three months when I went from almost family to almost single mom, growing my beautiful fish boy.

Get a malt, Doctor H said. Fries too.

Do you tell all your patients this? I asked because early on in my pregnancy when I was pounding on pounds, he suggested fewer fries and please no malts. This doctor who'd known me since high school, who turned tender protector when Kent died, who ordered an ultrasound (they weren't so common in 1987) to help me feel more connected to my boy, to help my boy feel more connected to me.

Still. The body changes. My body changed. My pre-baby flat stomach, mushy. My already big boobs, extra big when pregnant and nursing. Then hollow post-nursing. Boob sacs, one of my friends said about hers, about mine, and we both laughed.

Dressing up: leather skirt with fishnets and black ankle boots. In skin clothes that showed curves. Where I wasn't hiding. Breathing air back into my body. The squiggle of desire, in the brine of me. Skirt zipped to my spine. Leather is forgiving. I'd forgotten that. Added a tight top with a lace-up front, black bra peeking through. I spun left and right in the full-length mirror. Grateful to spy a little of before-grief me, reflecting back. If I narrowed my eyes, softened my gaze:

There I was.

I thought all my desire died on that mountain road with Kent.

I'd told myself I was okay with that. I was okay with no more belly flutters, no more wet between the legs, no more pulsing in the dip of my collarbones.

Then I watched Scot play. The blueness of his bass. His bass with its curves. The callouses on his fingertips. His fingers on strings. His fingers on me.

Singers are nice, the partner of the lead singer whisper-shouted to me one time when I was swooning over the singer's voice.

But bass players, she said, with a nod to Scot, to memory. Those hands, she said. Her sigh—whew—like blowing smoke through rounded lips.

I studied Scot. All grin and glow. Strumming his Lake Placid blue Fender bass. It felt like just us—him playing to me, me watching him—even though there was the rest of the band with the diva lead singer and the lead guitar player who spun his amp up a notch louder than Scot's. And the drummer who rushed a little even though Scot did his best to hold him, hold the steady. I wouldn't have heard the fraction of rush, but Scot told me. And once I heard it, I heard it every time.

Bass man. The underbeat. The glue. Steady. Of course he was a bass player. He'd been holding the bass line all his life. Playing the bass since he was 13, when his parents bought his first bass and amp, when they had the We need to know you're serious conversation, since money was tight.

What's your band's name? I asked on our first date.

Do You Want Fries with That? he said, and I busted out a laugh. It will long be my favorite name of his bass man bands.

What kind of music?

Mostly rock. Rolling Stones. Led Zeppelin.

Is rock your favorite?

I'm more jazz than rock, he said. The Blues. Motown. Funk. I nodded. I could see it. The heart of a jazz player. Where his soul shines.

I love Ray Charles, he said. "Georgia on My Mind"? Damn. So good.

Women want the lead, Scot said, several dates in when I'd gone to see him play when I did my best to be a groupie.

Playing the bass never got me a lot of action, he said and laughed, his eyes slitting behind aviator glasses.

Their oops, I said. I only want the bass player. Your luck is changing. Mine too.

Wet conductor. Lub dub bass beat. Tender thunder. Four chamber engine. Fifth chamber magic maker.

Boomerang heart. Boundless heart. Bendy too. Born of fire and sun. Cradles the loves the Greeks named: eros (passion), philia (friends), storge (parents for children), and agape (humankind). Loves beyond ocean and sky. Loves beyond infinity.

After

Can I help you with that? Scot asked as I tested the heat of Jake's bottle against the tender of my wrist.

I mean, I know you do all the stuff on your own, Scot added. But I'm here, he said with a half shrug. If you want.

I got it.

All right, he said, and I felt his eyes as I fumbled with hot water and warm bottle, as I fumbled with accepting his help.

I was galaxies from opening the door to my little family band. I couldn't admit then how scared I was to let anyone in, because what if I did, and they died too? Or what if I was too broken to pick another good one? Was I brave enough to risk losing love? Did I get to build a beautiful life? Or would the long arms of Kent and Widowed be my forever shadows.

I couldn't be honest with my mouth of fears, so I judged Scot, measured him against dead Kent. My list was long in the ways Scot wasn't: Not tall enough. Bark-brown hair, not slate grey. Beard a shade darker than his hair, not coyote brown with cinnamon streaks. Deep-ocean blue, not sky-blue eyes. Not a bass drum slow heartbeat. Not a physicist who loves poetry. Not a bookstore wanderer. Or a record collector. Not a German chocolate cake eater or Cherry Coke drinker. Not a fish and Brussels sprouts for breakfast breakfaster. Or pretend opera singer. Not a motorcycle rider. Not a carry me to bed guy. Not Kent.

Scot burrowed into the scratchy polyester plaid couch with its fake leather straps that girdled the moss-green and dirt-brown plaid like twine on hay bales. Him: one foot slouched on the opposite knee. Scuffed unwhite tennis shoes. Tube socks. Levi 501s. Irish-green and white-striped rugby shirt, hints of fray at the cuffs. Aviator glasses framed almost navy-blue eyes. Dark-brown hair like mine. Enough like mine, my over-the-fence neighbor, my Yoo-Hoo! neighbor, shouted from her side of the six-foot wooden fence: Yoo-hoo! Is that your brother I've seen around?

Maybe she wanted to be the first to know who the new guy was since I'd become a curiosity on my suburban cul-de-sac padded with young families. Driveways cluttered with sedans and station wagons and big bikes, little bikes. 1970s tri-level and two-story homes plotted in a crescent shape. Fir and maple trees. Pinecones and eggplant-colored leaves draped lawns in fall. My first home I bought with Kent, in the curve of the crescent: unhomed once he died.

My next-door neighbor John (always kindness and soft hellos) cut my grass without asking me. Sometimes it took me days to notice the grass haircut, buzzed and spiky. Other neighbors half-waved or skirted inside their homes like it was too much to see me. Maybe death was contagious. Maybe their hearts couldn't bear my thunder tears, my full-throated Fuck, fuck, fuck at the mower when it sputtered and wouldn't start. Maybe I was too hard to witness.

While I warmed Jake's nighttime bottle, Scot sank into the couch in my family room. Jake ditched his best stuffed animal, Cinnamon Bear, and inched toward Scot in that way of early walkers—tiny hands gripped the edge of the couch, knees locked, tuning his balance. Jake in his duckling-yellow footed jammies, fuzzy from overwashing. Jake's hazel eyes lasered on Scot. Jake in his determination to reach this man who'd slipped into our lives in a side-door way.

Someone's going to fall in love with your boy and then fall in love with you, Mom said months before, and alarm bloomed in my gut. My sisters nodded like sisters do.

One, I started, index finger pointed to the ceiling. There will be no more falling in love. I said those words and tears pooled in the cave of my throat.

Pretty sure no one gets a second love like I had, I said, before the women in my life could toss in their words. Lisa studied her Converse tennis shoes. Jan pursed ruby-red lips.

I swallowed hard against the soggy sponge in my throat feeling.

And two, I went, my fingers in a peace sign. If there is any falling in love, I slowed my words, hit *if* hard. It'll be far, far from now. And it's got to be me first, then Jakester.

Because. My boy was adorable. Pure love at the core of my cosmology. His laugh split the sky. Of course, anyone with a beating heart would fall for him. And me? I was a messy mess. Marinating in Grief's-a-Bitch days. Not ready to see grief's gifts, to see what I'd gained when I lost everything. Days bucketed in monsoon tears, scribbling in journals, smoking Marlboro Reds. Endless days of wearing the same black and white checked shirt. Grimy dishes. Sticky floors. Rotten vegies. Stacks of junk mail. I wasn't ready back when Mom said those falling in love words. I wasn't sure if I was ready yet.

As I heated Jake's bottle, I eyed my boy inching, inching, inching to Scot. Hand over hand, legs stiff, Jake navigated the length of the plaid couch until he reached his target. Then he patted Scot's knee.

Hi Jake, Scot said and smiled at my cub.

The sweetness of my boy.

These two.

I flashed on *my guys*.

Not yet, I thought. *Not yet.*

My stomach dipped then climbed my ribs. This sidecar of guilt. Disloyalty jabbed its sour punch a hand width above my belly button. Was my churning gut laced with that old story of my girl-promise that I'd never mess around outside marriage like my dad? Of course I wasn't cheating. And the body holds all the stories.

I breathed hard into my gut twist.

Thoughts spun and parked on: *Just the cub. My guy.*

Jake laughed his little boy laugh that gurgled from his toes up. He tapped, tapped Scot, his tiny fingers spread wide like palming an invisible baby basketball. Jake wedged himself between Scot's knees, balancing with one hand on each of Scot's thighs.

Jake's hazel eyes, some place between acorn and butterscotch, like my sister Lisa's. Wide. Circled by a shore of leggy lashes.

Jake stretched his arms up in a little big *V.* Open. Trust.

Want up? Scot asked.

Is it okay?

Sure, I said, one palm shoulder-high. He wants to sit with you.

Uuup, Scot said, scooping his voice and Jake. He landed Jake next to him, not on his lap, next to him, thigh to thigh, like friends. Jake clapped and laughed his rainbow laugh.

And my heart turned mush. Melty around the edges. The perfect campfire s'mores heart: gooey, sweet, delicious. Love cup: full. My truth spot pinged. Four fingers below my collarbone, on the curve of my heart.

I swiped misty eyes with my first knuckle. Crossing the room, I ignored the sea of baby blocks and books and stuffed Mickey Mouses and a Little Tikes car and toddler-sized kitchen with all its plastic food, while Jake studied me. Then he blinked at Scot like he was doing baby calculating. Jake could do this: flip from joy to serious. Flip. Snap. Contemplative baby. Light-hearted baby. Deep-thinker baby. He was all that and more from the moment he swam out of me.

Ready for your bottle, Bud? I asked, steps away from my cub and Scot.

Then.

Can I give him his bottle? Is it okay? Beard and mustache camouflaged his sliver smile.

My heart cramped. Campfire heart doused in a bucket of water. Hissing heart.

I'd breastfed him his first year. Bottles were newish. Only parents and sisters had fed my boy. Could I widen that circle?

My brain lit like fireflies swing-dancing on a sultry sweet summer night.

It's okay if you don't want me to, Scot said, his voice on low.

The woosh of heat as the furnace kicked on. I stared out the window at the falling down sun, papaya sky, fire sky as I stalled and side-barred with my heart as I listened to my heart whisper, *You can do this. It's okay. Let's take a chance.*

Handing Scot the warm bottle, my palm cooled.

These two. Side by side. Fuzzy yellow jammies to Levi's.

Scot angled the nipple toward Jake's mouth, but Jake shook him off and climbed in Scot's lap. He cupped his tiny hands around the warm milk, leaned into the crook of Scot's arm and guzzled, kicking one foot like he did. His lazy kick like he was dangling his foot off a dock.

An arcade game of feelings lit up, pinging and ponging just under skin: HappyConfusedUnsureHopefulScaredGrateful. Breath trapped between ribs. I told myself to breathe. I told myself: It's okay to turn toward your future and let the sun sun you. The center of my heart unclenched. The intersection of my four chamber heart with my heart's fifth chamber already rooted, already blooming, where more love, more kindness, more grace would home.

Thank you both, Scot said and smiled up from under his eyes. Brown bangs pushed to one side. Glasses a little slipped down.

This tenderness. His caution. It came from him naturally. There were things he understood from his own father loss. Father wound. Fatherless. Unfathered. Scot was 16 when his dad died. A boy cub. His mom remarried six months later and their grief talk dried up.

I moved in with cousins, he said, when he told me about his dad's sudden cancer death, how he died while Scot was driving to the hospital. How Scot drove his dad's empty steel-toed shoes home, untied.

I changed schools, he said. Mom gave me the '56 Chevy and a gas card. I drove a lot.

Grief Road in a '56 Chevy.

While his loss was different from mine, his woundedness gave him a sensitivity. Tender heart. Move with caution.

This is nice, Scot said, grinning at my darling boy cozy in his arms, all cuddly in his post-bath, winding down, melting into sleep time way, smelling like baby shampoo and goodness.

Did Jake smile behind his bottle? He did. That slurpy sound of lips off nipple, breaking the seal. Milk pooled in the corners of his mouth.

And me. I started to say something and stopped. I didn't have words.

And then Scot said the thing that almost undid me.

I just wish, for your sake. That your husband could be the one.

After

What's wrong? Tom asked, his hand on my forearm in *Stop*. I launched out of the molded plastic chair and in 10 mama steps reached Jake. Toddler Jake. All joy and wonder. Thrilled by Tom's backyard with eucalyptus and dappled sun. His backyard, a sea of kid hazards. Pavers. Rose thorns. A pool. A pool! With water and deep end and drowning.

Scot's right there, Tom said and pointed. He scratched his reddish beard, darker than his curly blond hair, with his not pointing hand. This heart friend I'd known since college. This friend who came and stayed with me in the early my-husband-died days. He flew up from San Diego. With me and my family as witness and comfort, in Be with. He didn't try to fix the unfixable. I carried his kindness in my marrow.

Jake and Scot laughed as they circled tiny circles around each other. Jake's shiny dark hair bouncing as he squealed. The tickle of grass on his bare toes. Scot barefoot too. When they stopped spinning and Scot turned his gaze away from Jake for a snap, my mama eyes lasered on Jake as he eyed the pool.

I was arms around my boy, swinging him to my hip, ignoring Tom's efforts to stop or at least slow me.

Scot seems like a good guy, Tom said, swatting the air on *good* and *guy*. The hole where he used to wear an earring blinked a tiny dark dot in the sun.

I wouldn't say that if I didn't see it, he added. You know I only want the best for you.

Isn't this what you wanted? he pushed. He already knew I did. He also knew it was hard for me to trust. Much as I longed to let go of my old story—People Who Love Me, Leave Me—sometimes it wrapped me in its gooey history.

I wanted to say, Of course it's what I want.

I wanted the tumble of love again.

I wanted to be thrilled to share Jake.

I wanted.

Thoughts pinged like hail on a barn roof. My left scapula pinched. My shame spot. This shame I felt for wanting, for not being able to voice my wants, not trusting myself, not knowing how to put my broken parts back together.

And more.

If I let go of being The One for Jake, would I lose myself again? Here's the thing.

Jake was my way back from the night sky. Heartline. Loveline. This tug of boy flooded my heart with joy and hope. He lassoed me from the echo of deep space. His double helix genes in me. Mine in him. This call beyond words. In the belly of grief when all I saw was loss and uncertainty, I wrapped that loveline around my waist and hauled myself in through galaxies of dark.

Then Scot arrived at the shore of my heart. Scot who wanted to be part of our little family duo. Who wanted three-ness from two-ness, too.

Could I risk my heart?

After

When couple to family turned out to be a family of two, not three, my longing swallowed me. I ached for our straight line of two to be a pointy triangle of three. I saw threes everywhere.

Beginning. Middle. End.

Three graces: charm, beauty, and creativity.

In numerology three is the synthesis, the offspring of one and two. Three calls on humans to remember we carry divinity within.

The number of bones in the human ear.

Cerberus: the three-headed dog in mythology that guards the gates of the Underworld, allowing the dead to enter but none to leave.

Bronte sisters.

Strands of a braid.

Maiden, mother, crone.

Proton, neutrons, electrons.

Third eye.

Lithium: third element on the periodic table.

Christian Holy Trinity.

Rule of three: groups of three are more effective.

Waltz.

Triplets.

Triple Crown.

Macbeth witches.

Shakespeare, Keats, Dickinson.

Pavarotti, Placida, Carreras.

In East and Southeast Asia there's a superstition that it's unlucky to take a photo with three people. It's professed that the person in the middle will die first.

The Christmas before Kent died, when my baby belly was a halfmoon, a cousin took family portrait pictures at our extended-family Christmas. I didn't feel beautiful or glowy like people say about pregnant women. More like a shiny fuzzball of pink satin in the one dressy maternity thing I owned.

We could skip it, I told Kent.

Up to you, he said.

Take your picture, Dad urged. You'll be glad later.

When Kent died on January 13th, it's one of the few things I asked: Who has those pictures from the Christmas party?

Dad stared at something over my head. Then sucked breath in between his teeth like he did when he needed a moment.

Something was wrong with the camera. I'm so sorry, he said, his hazel eyes with his one droopy lid stared straight at me as he jiggled loose coins in his pocket.

After

I s he toad number one? Liz asked about Scot as she swirled her vanilla latte counterclockwise.

I'd told my widow friends I needed to kiss five toads—not in that boring trope of toads-to-princes. More like experimenting. More like a one-off. I'd need to kiss and fuck at least five men before I could imagine giving one my heart.

Is he? Liz asked.

Not sure, I said. Maybe not.

I thought about (pre-Scot) me telling Emily I wouldn't date. Then telling her if I did date, the guy would have to be completely different from Kent, nothing in common with the man who'd loved me bigger than the sky. So you're going to date an asshole? she asked back then, and I couldn't have loved her more.

And now, here I was, dating Scot. This man carved from kindness. Smart and funny and soulful. Fiercely loyal. Patient. Qualities I loved in Kent too.

How'd you guys do it? I asked and eyed the other widows in our amoeba-shaped circle. How'd you date? How'd you fall in love? Wait. How'd you let yourself fall in love? I asked.

What I wanted to know: How'd you get past the fear?

Maddie rubbed her arthritic hands together, her index finger at an angle at the first knuckled. She flicked off some lunch crumbs.

It didn't happen all at once, and it kinda did, she said right after. Her cheeks cheeked up in their moon-face way.

Since I'd been happy once, Maddie went. I was pretty sure I could be happy again. I am pretty sure I can be happy again.

Were you scared? I asked and willed myself to sit still, not slap my flip-flops against my heels.

Sure. Absolutely. So scared.

Beth and Sarah and Liz nodded Yes along with Maddie's words. The blonde and brunette of them in head bobs like widow Slinkies, slinking in sync.

Remember when I met Maddie that first time at group and said I hated her? I wasn't inspired. Remember? She said she was single and going on a date. I wasn't ready to hear that then.

Sitting in our close widows' circle, I was grateful to be ready to hear more life, more love was possible. Maybe not all at once. Maybe in micro moments.

We all were dating. Me, the most recent.

I eyed them like I used to eye my big sis. Watching her put on makeup. Baby-blue eye shadow was the wow shade then. Watching her tie orange and yellow and red scarves. Sometimes around her neck. Sometimes her head. I studied her. Wanted to be like her.

I could follow these women who'd been carving their ways in the grief woods. I trusted them as I was learning to trust myself.

I don't think Scot's a toad, I said.

But I'll kiss him some more and let you all know.

After

S ee this shape? the astrologer asked, her pencil poised above
my natal chart: a star map of what the cosmos looked like
when I pushed through into this life.

My chart with lines in squares and triangles, marked with
yellow, red, blue, and green lines. Like the Spirograph drawings
I made as a girl, when I'd pin down the outer cog, fit a smaller
cog in the bigger one, and follow the pattern. I'd draw in primary
colors. I'd freehand shapes in black ink over the geometric Spirograph shapes.

It's a fixed cross, the astrologer said and tucked her pewter
hair behind her ear.

I didn't know what that meant. And I told her.

Think about a crucifix, she started.

I waited.

In astrology it's a sign of opposites.

Like a crossroad?

Different, she said. Not an either/or, which is how we often
think of crossroads.

I pursed my lips, hummed that hmmm sound in my throat.

When it's in your chart, it means you're able to hold opposites at the same time.

That pinging I feel four fingers below my collarbone when I hear a truth: it pinged, pinged. This pulsing over my heart. My north star.

Think of it like this too—you're both this and that, she said. You're that and this.

All of it.

One doesn't eclipse the other.

I've always been that way, I said as muscles over my heart tightened and tears leaked out the corners of my eyes.

I thought I was being indecisive, I said, tears amping up.

You were born this way, the astrologer assured. Her voice tumbled like river water.

It's a gift, she said. To be able to hold opposites. To hold the light and the dark.

I stared at my chart with its circles and lines. With its angles and squares and triangles. With its cross. The map of me. I thought about grief: how grief is joy and sorrow holding hands. How it's me at the intersection.

I looked out her window at the massive oak in her yard, leaves and branches branching up, roots rooting down. All we see above ground. All we don't see below dirt.

And with all our gifts, she started. There's the underside.

Breath caught between top ribs. What's the opposite of opposites?

You want to accomplish everything at once, she said.

I let out a laugh that sounded more like a hiccup. Tipped my head toward my shoulder and grinned.

That's true too, I said. I always figured it's Sagittarius-me. Shooting arrows. Taking chances.

Oh, it is, she said. And in you it's *extra* extra because of this cross.

Do you ever have trouble figuring out where to start?

Body chills flared in my elbows and knees, flooded arms and legs and chest and belly and pelvis, crept to my ears.

All the time. All the time. All the time.

After

A re you sure you want to be with me? I asked, words arrowed past the windshield at the sunflower sun.

What? Scot said and I could feel him sit up, his spine stack-straight.

What are you trying to say? A crack of silence.

Then.

Of course I do. Why would you ask that? he said, his voice a little stumbly, his steadiness leaking.

It's just that—I started and squished my lips like I did sometimes before I said something big—it's, well, Kent was married to Claire and Claire died. Then Kent married me and he died.

This hard knot under my bone cage, like I'd swallowed a peach pit.

Don't you worry it's my turn? I said in a rush. Don't you worry I'll die next?

Scot reached across the bench seat of my Taurus station wagon and grabbed my hand. Pulled it to lips and kissed the back, the palm, the palm again while I breathed, while I slowed my giddy-up heart.

Remember in *The World According to Garp*? When the airplane crashes into the house just as they're buying it?

I nodded tiny nods. Felt tears at the cones of my eyes.

Remember how Garp says, We'll take it!? Because the chances of another plane hitting are outrageous, or something like that? That's how I look at it. You've had your disaster. Now maybe you're disaster proof.

I wanted to believe him. Bad. I liked his Garp logic.

The world according to Scot? I asked.

Yup.

I clicked my bracelet open, shut, open, shut. Chewed my bottom lip.

Being widowed doesn't make me feel like it will never happen again, I started. Actually, it could, I said. My words splintered and stabbed my throat.

I'm not immune. No one is.

We listened to the hum of wheels on the road, the bump bump of the car over neighborhood speed bumps.

It's a chance I'm taking, he said.

I know there are no guarantees.

But I think Garp knew something, he added and kissed my hand again.

After

I had that dream.

In waking life I was getting to know Scot, letting him in our little family band, following my heart that thrummed and thundered: Scot.

In sleeping life there was Kent.

I move from the too-white hall into Jake's bedroom with teddy bears and alphabet blocks tumbling on the wallpaper border I glued up one winter afternoon.

There you are, Kent says. I've been looking for you.

I spill an armful of laundry: Tiny T-shirts and pants and blankets and sheets plunk to the rust-orange carpet. Baby socks roll like they're battery powered.

You're here, I say, my heart twittering like a caught feral animal.

You're here.

I want to race to him, but my feet are concrete in that stuck dream way.

I'm so happy to see you.

Kent smiles. Tents his left eyebrow and lowers his right. Checkmark brow. Whatcha doin' brow. He picks up one of Jake's blankets and unfolds it. Holds it at arm's length with a snap. Folds it in half and in half again.

What are you doing? I ask.

Folding blankets, he says, casual, like this is what he does on the regular, and why am I surprised?

Weren't they folded?

Yeah, but not very well, he says as he plucks another from the folded pile and refolds it—a blue crocheted blanket a friend of his mom's crocheted with crooked fingers and a tender heart.

It's laundry, he says as he restacks the blankets. You know I'm in charge of laundry.

Next he straightens Jake's shoes: white walking shoes, salt-water sandals, red tennis shoes with red rubber toes. He lifts the toddler-sized shoes off their shelf, sets them on the changing table, places them back where he found them.

I've been doing the laundry, I say, my voice like rocks in a tumbler.

But it's my job, he says. And I know I'm behind.

He grins at me with his Siberian Husky blue eyes and the crabby that was climbing my chest into my throat, that was almost past my teeth, melts. This receding tide of hurt and longing.

I've missed you, I say, my ache so loud it pounds in my ears.

I know, Kent says. I have to go now.

But— I start. Don't go, I plead. Please. My feet unstick and I launch across the room, sling my arms around my beloved. My chest fuses to his.

I love you.

I love you too, he says. You were my one true thing.

Stay, I say, because I know I'm in dreamworld and I know where these dreams go.

I keep my ear plastered to his chest, afraid to see his face, afraid to see he's turning to shadow like I know he will.

I have to go, he says as his body melts. A pile of slushy snow covers my bare feet, my chipped Tiffany Blue nail polish.

Don't! I scream as I race out of Jake's room, down the stairs, yank open the metal front door, the one I'd spied the chaplain through the night Kent died and the hand-wringing chaplain woke me up.

In the driveway. Our mangled Honda Prelude. Punched through from the right headlight to the rear left fender. Splashed in blood red.

I woke to tears, my heart and breath jammed in my throat. Gasping.

Just me in my bed.

Just me clinging to sheets.

Just me.

I whispered on repeat what I'd been practicing saying, even though I wasn't sure I believed yet: His death was his own. It had nothing to do with me.

Before

Gina threw a shoe! I told Dad when he asked why I was pounding a stick between two rocks. Me, imagining myself as a farrier, fixing my horse's thrown horseshoe. Cool night air. Cloudless sky. Round moon. Man in the Moon winking. Stars like spilled glitter. The milky of the Milky Way. Me cool to the night. Hot to the fire that snapped and spit. This bonfire at our family ranch. Yellow and orange flames licked the black sky. Dad and aunts and uncles and grandparents on metal lawn chairs with fabric woven seats, perched around the fire pit. Cousins chased around the fire, played swords with their not-burning sticks, asked for more marshmallows. Mama in the trailer with baby sis. Mama who was all city girl and would want me to take a bath when I came in, but I'd crawl inside my sleeping bag with pictures of horses on the flannel lining and fall asleep to the tumble sound of Mama running the bath.

She what? But the farrier's gone, Dad said and mumbled God-damnit, while my church-going Nana said, in the same breath as him, David! No swearing.

I jammed my fist in my mouth to keep from laughing since Granddad swore all the time. All the goddamn time.

It's okay, I said. I'll fix it.

Bam. Bam. Bam.

I pounded the hot, cooling, hot, cooling stick some more, shaping it like I watched the farrier do earlier, with fire and anvil and hammer, making a new shoe for my horse, Gina. I pushed hair out of my face, loose strands from my now messy ponytail. After fire time, when I go in the trailer, under the too-bright lights, I'll have a smear of charcoal across my cheek that I will love, and Mama will want to wash off.

Hey Number Two, Dad started (He called us by our numbers sometimes: big sis Number One, me Number Two, little sis Number Three) you know you can't make horseshoes from sticks, right?

I poked my stick back in the fire. I closed my eyes and imagined Gina's hoof so I could get her shoe just right. That bend in the center. The way the ends faced each other and didn't touch.

You and your imagination, Dad said and clicked another beer open.

When the fire next jumped to my stick that I had jammed in the heat, at the base where the fire was orange, I yanked it out and wrote my name against the night sky: Annie, Annie, Annie. All in cursive. One long Annie. I wrote fast so I could watch the stick glow against the star-pierced sky. This sky that was mine. This sky I marked as my own.

After

Sometimes I wish Kent would walk through the door, back into my life, I started, wondering if I was alone in my magical thinking. I scanned the faces of the other widows. This circle of women who held my story, who held my heart. They all nodded, *Yes, me too*. Maddie bowed her curly head.

I mean, it'd be a little weird now that Scot's in my life, I went, but we'd figure it out. A sound some place between a laugh and grunt zipped out of me.

And weirder, I think Scot and Kent would like each other.

I said those words and got chills because yes, those two would like each other. They were similar in temperaments: kind and loving and funny. Loyal beyond loyal. I felt a gush of gratitude and love. A gush of second chances can be beautiful even when splashed with a sidecar of doubt.

Am I moving backwards? I asked.

While I didn't believe in the five stages people used to talk about grief (denial, bartering, anger, depression, acceptance), while I believed in Before and After as my grief markers, I was still looking for proof that I was growing in grief, that grief made me bigger—not smaller. And then I'd have these wishing moments when I longed for Kent, and my beliefs that grief had taught me a wider compassion, a deeper love, felt like shriveled hope—not belief.

Not backwards, Emily offered. Grief isn't linear. Hearts are complex.

When it hits, it's still super painful, Beth said, tucking an escaping curl behind her ear. I still get knocked down. I just get up faster than I used to.

I still get mad that for the rest of my life, I don't get to have Steve, Sarah said, and a sigh the size of the room escaped her strawberry lips. I get all the memories and I don't get to make new ones. At some point I'll miss him for longer than I had him.

That last thing Sarah said: missing him for longer than she had him? That hit hard. My eyes stung and fuzzed with tears. At nine years older than me, Kent was always going to be older. Now, if I was lucky, I'd catch up. If I was lucky, I'd get older than he'd ever be.

As I stretched for a Kleenex, Liz said: I tell friends I haven't moved on and I have moved forward. She sucked her cheek on one side for a beat. And yup, some days I still wish AJ would walk through the door. Maybe what's changed is that I don't actually expect him to.

Grief bound us. Grief as mosaic—dream robber to mentor with snarly paths along the way. No timelines. No prescriptions. No being over grief. No right way, no wrong way to navigate. And while the hard parts almost undid us, we all agreed we'd grown as humans: more compassion, more love. Grief as superpower came from being with grief, feeling it all, hunting for joy and beauty when hunting felt right, not looking for rainbows when that felt right too.

After

My anger boiled. Bubbled out.

See the crabby lady at the grocery store snapping, Don't bruise the tomatoes! at the bagger even though that bagger was a kid, a tube of acne cream in his hip pocket.

Or the fussy woman at the dry cleaners complaining the stain still showed.

The unhinged human swearing at her lawnmower because she couldn't start it and she had oceans of grass that wouldn't stop growing.

The pissed-off gal who flipped you off because she had to slam on the brakes to keep from hitting you when you changed lanes with a sliver of space.

The wild woman who slowed but didn't stop, yelled: Out of my way! Her voice a fist, as she drove half off the road past construction workers with their stop signs flashing Stop.

I was all those.

More.

I wasn't mad. I was a mass of rage. Black fire. Underground burn. Cannonball water.

Rage with no good outlet. Who was I mad at? Kent. God. Life. Me. No crystal ball.

What did I know about honest feelings?

Dad's rage was sizzle burn boom. There was the time at the ranch when I was eight or nine. Just me and Dad in the trailer one evening. Him and vodka in his favorite tall, amber-colored plastic cup, ice cubes rubbing. He normally watched the news or Lawrence Welk, but that night he let me pick: *Mr. Ed* and *My Favorite Martian*. My stomach all swirly when he barked at the end of a show, What do you want to watch now? slurred to Whatcha wannn no-ow, as he refilled and refilled his cup behind the open cupboard, like maybe I couldn't see the gallon-sized Smirnoff bottle with its gallon-sized handle.

I snuck off to the bedroom shared with my sisters where our bunk beds were stacked three high. Big sis on top. Me in the middle. Little sis on the bottom. Eyed my fully packed white Samsonite suitcase with the powder-blue silky lining. Crawled in my middle bunk. Cuddled my stuffed lion with its matted hair. Fished my blue marble (the one that looked like the world) out of the zipper pocket in the back of Lizzy Lion and cupped it between my squeezed-together hands. I might have licked it. Then zipped my sleeping bag with pictures of horses grazing on the lining. Zipped it high to hide my cantering heart.

When Dad staggered by my hollow, trailer-thin door, he kicked it—hard. Kicked it with, Goddamnit. That tinny door flew open, smacked the wall, shook the wall mirror, and bounced back.

Ancestral wounds and stories rivered through DNA and beached on me.

Angry-me tossed out Kent's collection of magazines, the ones I used to tease him I'd donate to a library if he ever died before me. I regretted those words even though I knew they had nothing to do with him dying. I jammed the trash with *Scientific American* and *Smithsonian* and *Popular Mechanics* since it was pre-recycle days. I sold his boxes of *Time* magazines because I found a collector who hoped for the 1975 issue with Bruce Springsteen on the cover. You gotta take them all, I said. I hope you find The Boss.

I loaded my curbside trash can with boxes of mystery parts excavated from the garage: car parts, sockets and electrical parts, boxes of wires and washers and bits like puzzle pieces I didn't have manuals for.

I broke things.

That video I fished out of Kent's bottom desk drawer. That sticky drawer. The video squirreled between layers of Scientific Notation notebooks. His hiding place. That skin video. Women with dicks on the cover. Not strap-ons. Flesh dicks. Or men with boobs. Or humans in transition. Bodies in between. Whole bodies. Not broken. Just different from me. I didn't know. I didn't have the vocabulary.

My skin turned ice when I uncovered his porn.

Puke in the dark of my throat.

I crushed the secret skin video with a mallet. A hammer. Crushed it with rage in my stomping feet. Asking, Why couldn't you tell me? I wished you'd told me this was a thing for you, a turn on.

I broke things. Kent's things from his first wife. Unearthed in a garage purge. Keepsakes he burrowed away.

Who dies and leaves their wife with their dead wife's shit? I didn't understand keeping boxes of Halloween costumes, macramé plant hangers, googly eyes, stacks of felt. Boxes of romance novels. More. Boxes marked "Miscellaneous" in Kent's distinctive engineer-style printing.

A blow to my heart.

A throat full of jealous. A cauldron of hurt and mad and envy. What was I really mad at?

Were Kent and Claire together? When Kent's dad called Claire's mom to say the huge sad thing, to say he'd died, that's what her mom said: At least they're together. Those mom words haunted me, seared a hot poker hole in my heart.

I wanted to be all gracious and accepting that spirit life is a different life and whether they were or weren't didn't matter.

I wanted to have compassion for her, for him, for the way Kent blamed himself that her car crashed, blamed himself since he knew the tires were bad, blamed himself even though she knew the tires were almost hairless too.

I wanted to believe Ram Dass: We're all just walking each other home.

Yeah, I wanted that.

But I was small hearted.

I was all fury when I loaded my red Ford Ranger truck with my dead husband's dead-wife stuff: photos, lace, baby shoes (whose?), glue and pompoms and scissors. Boxes of romance novels with their cover shots of women's heads pitched back, breasts not quite showing. Boxes of earthenware dishes with muted yellow borders and cornflower-blue bouquets in the center.

The fury of me. Unhooked.

After

I backed my little red Ford Ranger pickup up to the metal trough at the dump. No driving out to heaps of garbage like when I was a girl. Dumping was sanitized here. Instead of heaps of stinky garbage, you flung everything into a metal trough with a conveyor that scooted garbage out of sight.

I backed my truck up, turned off the engine, and climbed into the bed. Then hefted the first box of Claire memories.

Had Kent packed Claire's stuff like I packed a Kent box for Jake to open when he's older? When I cranked up James Taylor, smoked a cigarette before combing through Kent's memorabilia/mementos/memories. When I chose Kent objects, wrapped and tucked them in a record-sized box. Jake was a few months old, sleeping a long nap, while I sorted and packed what I imagined as a future archeological dig. When I weighed each item, how each piece told a story, made a human. Can we know another through their objects? Does a little stardust stay behind on the things our beloveds touched?

As I chose each keepsake, I imagined Jake opening the box as a teenager or older. I pictured stories paired with everything: pictures (Little Kent in cowboy boots. Kent grinning with blue ribbons at science fairs. Teen Kent with his first backpack. Then with his parents, his sister and her family. Kent in the woods. Lone Kent on a boulder in Yosemite overlooking the valley), diplomas, report cards, newspaper clippings, science fair prizes. T-shirts washed and folded one more time ("Blue Angels", "Dinosaur Days", "People in Seattle Don't Tan They Rust"), baseball mitt, polished geode, straight-edge razor and strap that Kent actually shaved with, slide rule, mini Norton motorcycle, black leather wallet with its worn edges.

My chest squeezed weighing Claire boxes to the Kent box. Then not. They weren't the same.

I'd crafted a memorial. A portal for Jake to know his Dad in ways maybe I'd forget to say over time as memory fuzzed up. A portal rooted beneath memory. Memory. That shape-changer we alter each time we revisit the experience. While our brain's hippocampus acts as a card catalog or search engine, pointing us to the original event, each time we touch memory, we alter it, remembering the last time we visited it, drifting farther from the actual experience. While I longed to keep Kent memories true, I also knew it was impossible.

Kent didn't pack Claire boxes with the same intent. Her boxes said more about Kent's save-and–reuse-everything world view. The craft bits leftovers from her teaching preschool. I bet he'd imagined donating all those googly eyes.

For me they became a perfect rage outlet.

Good-fucking-bye! I shouted as I heaved a craft box packed with pom-poms, googly eyes, felt, bric-a-brac, feathers, beads, sequins. The box thudded—bam!—against the metal trough with its conveyor belt swishing junk away. Bye-bye lace and Halloween costumes too.

Good-fucking-bye!

Paperbacks next. Three fruit-sized boxes. The size produce people unload at the supermarket.

Paperbacks. Covers with women, their heads thrown back, exposing necks, chest, and a hint of cleavage. I twisted and hurled one, two, three boxes in the dumping space. I breathed hard with the last box. Sweat trickled down my spine into the waist of my jeans.

Why'd you keep her books? I yelled with each heave.

Why?

I breathed harder and stared down the last two boxes in the bed of my truck. Cream-colored dishes. Service for what, 12? I discovered them two years before.

What about these? I asked Kent when I found them buried in the labyrinth of our garage.

Oh, they were our everyday dishes, he said. Claire's and mine.

And what do you want to do with them? I asked, hoping he'd say pitch them, wanting to stay neutral in my asking while my belly did a little dip and dive.

Look. I know you don't like them. But they're decent, he said as he tucked them back on a shelf.

In the bed of my red Ranger, rage and betrayal boiled in me. My belly on fire. Flames flicked out my fingertips.

I opened the first box and threw three salad plates, Frisbee style. They slammed against the metal, crackling and splintering.

How could you leave me with ugly dishes? I yelled. I hate these dishes!

Adrenaline raced out fingers, toes, the crown of my head. Throat ached with tears and words. Swearing cut loose like teen-me. Stringing together swears: goddamnmotherfuckingallthe-fucksdishes. Fuckthedishes. Fuckthedishes. Fuckthedishes.

Fists of swearing.

Rage below rage.

Uncaged. All the times I wouldn't get mad at Kent because he didn't want to die. The ways I'd held back.

Who goes night skiing when their wife is pregnant? Who drives too fast on a snowy mountain road? Who doesn't turn around?

How could you leave me! I screamed. And all my Before spilled out too. A cauldron of hurt. Boiling. Popping. Hissing. Then.

Something cracked.

All the times I'd asked, Why me?

Something broke loose and I asked: Why not me?

A wedge of light seeped in, a whisper. A tiny fissure in my chest. Right at my thumping heart. I imagined grabbing hold of this sliver of light and tearing it open to what was behind, like standing in front of dusty old brocade curtains with light sneaking through. Handfuls of heavy drapes in each hand, I peeled back those weighty curtains, revealing a view. Tall green trees, thick with spring leaves, thorny underbrush, marshy emerald-green grass. An arc of trees mostly eclipsed a river that wandered behind it, a sandbar past the river, the ocean beyond the sand bar. Ocean licked the shore. The sun shone. Whitecaps.

Rooted in the bed of my red Ford Ranger, legs redwood tree strong—not young sapling—a forest tree with roots deep to the earth, a straight trunk, my arms, head, and hair turned to branches and leaves whistling in wind, drinking in the canary sun.

Alive. Not dead. Not husband. Me. Alive. This view in me. Me in this view.

My cells twitched with a knowing—joy and happy would be mine again. Hope. A wedge of hope calmed my dragon storm.

Right at the center of my heart, the fifth chamber swelled, bloomed brighter, bloomed me into a full-body grin.

I laughed at my empty truck bed. At the dappled light splashing the bench seat. At leaf shadows. Grinned at the You Can voices in me. How Grandma Sally said, You have to build your own garden. How Aunt Jean applauded me on tiptoe when I was reaching up: You got more in you, Sugar. You can.

I can.

I wiped dirty hands on my jeans, dusted off the fingerprints on my thighs, climbed back in the cab of my little red truck and drove home, singing/yelling "Don't Stop Believin'"—full tilt—the flaxen sun streaming in through the windshield.

After

Two days after going to the dump, after dumping Claire's craft bobbles, her books, and Halloween costumes. After breaking all those dishes and cracking myself open. After seeing me in those dish shards. After meeting myself in the darkest dark, in the mess of me, and not turning away. After singing all the way home and letting joy pulse through my body, the wonder and magic of it, since I thought I'd never feel joy again.

I'm so glad I was wrong. About that never feeling joy part.

Two days later I was back with my widow squad. Driving there, fingers drumming the steering wheel along with John Hiatt, singing "Have a Little Faith in Me," I imagined I'd be the first to share, to tell them about me at the dump, tell them how I broke apart and came together.

Natalie's joining us today, Emily said when I stepped in the waiting area. Remember, I told you all about her?

It felt weird and not weird to have a new member, to not be the newest.

A blip ago I was the new one. Scared to join a group where they knew each other and their stories. Not wanting to be part. Desperately wanting to be part.

Even though I knew suffering was not a competition, it was hard not to compare myself to the other widows then. They combed their hair. Their socks matched. Their clothes didn't look like they'd plucked them from a heap on the floor. Not me. I had to remember to smell my clothes before I yanked them on and, honestly, I forgot plenty. One of my depression faces looked like this: wear the same flannel shirt for a month. When the weather warms, switch to a T-shirt.

This is Natalie, Emily said and smiled at the blonde with amber eyes, dressed in a mustard-yellow jumpsuit with oversized turquoise jewelry. Earrings, bracelet, necklace—all matching. When her blonde hair looked salon fresh and she smelled like Amazing Grace—a once upon a time favorite perfume—I counted on grief fingers and guessed she'd been widowed longer than I was.

Hi, Natalie said, her eyes roving the circle. Each of us—Liz, Maddie, Beth, Sarah, and me—nodded and smiled.

Let's introduce yourselves today with your name and how long you've been widowed, Emily said. Then we can jump in.

Huh?

No Dead Husband Story?

My fault lines quivered.

How would I get to know her if I didn't know her story? If I didn't hear howwhenwhywasitsuddenwasitnothow her husband died?

Natalie in matching jewelry, makeup, and combed hair. I guessed she'd swam in the ocean of grief and found some shore.

I couldn't have been more wrong.

It'd been a few months.

Did my mouth go to *O* when she said that?

Putting myself together helps me feel together, she said as though she could hear inside my head.

But sometimes it backfires, she said, patting her turquoise necklace, that gorgeous shade of blue like a piece of sky fell to the earth. People see me and assume I'm better, which is miles from the truth. I might look pulled together, but really I'm falling apart.

She went on to tell us how after her husband died she cleaned out his clothes, then couldn't stand his empty drawers, so she filled them with jewelry. Everything in sets.

That way it's easy to get dressed. I open a drawer and pick a color, she said and spread her arms wide like Maddie had the first time I came to group when she announced she was single and going on a date.

Everyone grieves how they grieve, Emily said, and our heads shot up and down, in *Yes* and *Yes* and *Yes.*

When it was my turn, I told them about the dump.

Damn it felt good to let myself be mad. I bet I looked unhinged out there, throwing craft crap and books and dishes, I said, sucking in a big breath before I went on. I didn't care. I don't care. The only thing better would have been to burn it all in a bonfire.

I burned all my lingerie one day, Liz said. Boy, does nylon smoke. She made a sound between a guffaw and a hiccup as she flipped her hair behind her shoulder.

I burned his car magazines, Beth said, her mossy green eyes bright. The whole big stack.

Isn't it cathartic? I've always burned things, I said. I've loved fire since I can remember.

Such a good way to purge, Sarah added, smoothing her wrinkleless pant leg.

I need to do some burning, Maddie said. The light in her blue eyes amped up. I hadn't thought about it before. Burning, I mean.

I love our group, Maddie added. If we had a name, what would it be?

A Band of Burners.

Burn It Down.

Widows on Fire.

Say It Loud.

Say It Now.

After

Idon't want to be in a relationship, Natalie said, running fingers through her blonde, wavy hair. Amber eyes flitted from widow face to widow face.

We'd barely settled into our circle at group time. She threw that down first thing.

But I miss sex, she said. I just want a wind-up guy I can have sex with, then he can go back to his corner.

That's called a dildo, I said, and we all laughed.

I just want someone for me, Natalie started on another Tuesday. Not my kids. Matt was the best dad. No one can replace him. He'll always be their dad, she said, worrying her bracelet, the brick-red one that matched her brick-red earrings and necklace.

The rest of us were dating, glad to be dating, not-glad to be dating.

This whole dating thing, Sarah sighed and crossed her legs, thigh over thigh. I go from teen butterflies to being mad at Steve again. I'm lousy at dating! She swung her foot, tapping air. But I liked being married, she said, softer. And I'd like it again. Wish I didn't feel so disloyal.

My gut thrummed at *disloyal*. My vision of Greek widows flooded me. The culture: once widowed, stay widowed. I'd seen them in Greece when I traveled as a college student. Women all dressed in black, spines curled, bodies turned to commas, this pause, this breath between life and death, a pause from here to there to where not here. How Greek was I? Could I be Greek in the ways I loved, a deep and wide pride in my heritage, without being too Greek in the widow way?

Emily looked from face to face to face, a silent opening for who else?

I feel guilty, I said. Not all the time, thank the stars. Late at night when I'm alone and missing Kent, guilt pops in. My breath caught a little in the basement of my throat, saying those words. I waited a beat for my left scapula to ping and it didn't.

Then I think about Kent and I know he'd find another partner if I'd died before him, I said, my nose pinching like it does before tears. He'd always love me and he wouldn't stay in grief.

This round of yups and yesses. Crossed arms uncrossed. Bodies leaned in.

When I think of Steve, Sarah started, I know he'd want me to be in a relationship. She pressed hands to thighs, her fingernails bubble gum pink. But it's tricky, she went. Keeping him with us, moving forward, taking him with us, not taking him with us.

Yup, Beth spoke up. One of my friends who meant well said recently, Oh, if Sean died I'd never remarry. He's my everything. Then she caught herself. Gawd, I'm sorry, she said. I mean *me*, she said. It's different for you.

Ouch. Maddie massaged her swollen knuckles. People have no idea what they'd do. I used to think the same thing—that I'd never remarry. And here I am. She grinned that grin that lit her face and rounded her round cheeks. Carl wouldn't want me to stay single, she said. I don't want me to stay single.

I don't want a dad for my kids, Natalie said, circling back to where she started. I mean, they've had the best. Matt will always be their dad.

I thought of my stepdad—my second dad. He'd been dad to my sisters and me since I was 10. The one who was there to tell us to stop when little sis and I fought over doing the dishes each night, who was there to teach us how to change the oil in our cars, to tell us not to wear too much perfume, to talk about reincarnation.

What if your kids get another adult who loves them? I asked.

Natalie crossed her arms, tipped her pelvis back, twitched her jaw.

As soon as I said it, I wanted the words back.

Or not, I said. Or not.

What matters is what you each want, Emily said, leaning in. What do you want?

Someone for me, Natalie repeated. I mean, of course I want him to be kind to my kids, but I don't want him to be part of making decisions, or finances, or any parenting. She tapped fingers to thigh with each declaration.

I thought about her wanting a wind-up man, a dick-in-the-corner man.

I'm just going to be clear from the start with anyone I date, she said. There are plenty of men who don't want to parent.

True. Families, like the people in them, take all kinds of shapes.

And my kids are adamant, Natalie said, flicking the stretchiness of her bracelet. They don't want a stepdad. They're struggling enough. Did I tell you my daughter wrote an essay for English class titled, "My Death Life"? Gawww.

I'd read it, I said.

Of course you would, she said and touched my forearm, pink nails against my tanned skin. Thank you.

I was the one who brought books to our group. Me, searching for grief words, for grief balms. I'd shared *When Bad Things Happen to Good People* by Harold Kushner, *A Grief Observed* by C.S. Lewis, and *In the Midst of Winter: Selections from the Literature of Mourning*. It was years before Joan Didion had her heart splitting grief and wrote *The Year of Magical Thinking*, or I would have shared that too.

I love that your kids all express their grief, I said, looking for a beat at each widow warrior. These women I had nothing but awe and respect for.

I wonder what it will be like for Jake, how his grief will be for him.

Thank god for therapy and Emily, Liz said. I don't know what my family would have done without her. I mean, it's still messy, but this— she made her arms wide like a huge hug from your favorite aunt—this saved us.

Most of the kids of the widows had seen or were seeing Emily. I always listened with my whole body when they talked about their kids' grief. Me wondering how Jake would grieve down the road. How do you grieve a parent you never met? I'd be open however his grief showed up. Grief wasn't a secret. His would be his, like mine was mine.

This was group time. Sometimes we stayed with a topic: guilt, disloyalty, the heartburn of stitching a new life. And sometimes we pinged all over. It was always right. It was always good. These women. They're how I saved myself.

Before

I did it! I shouted to treetops, to mountain air so pure I hiccupped when I gulped it, to seersucker-blue sky.

I did it! I shouted to clouds round as snow cones with flat bottoms, like they'd been plunked on a grill then dropped in the sky. Me. At the Continental Divide, 11,000 feet above the sea. One dusty boot in the west. One in the east. Me at my fault lines. Me after two weeks of hiking through deep woods. No trails. No paths. Forest thick with downed trees. With evergreens. With the crunch of needles and branches. Bushwhacking through underbrush that scraped and tugged my calves and thighs. That scraped and tugged my grit.

Then. My body in a capital X. My voice a hammer shouting, I did it! Me and my bruised, pummeled, mosquito chewed, sunburned, stinky, muscle strong body. Me and my greasy hair, hairy legs, bushy pits, and wild brows. Me and my heart.

I straddled the Continental Divide and remembered Nike, Winged Victory of Samothrace, who welcomes all at the top of the Daru staircase in the Louvre. I'd seen her in college. Gawked at her gorgeous female form, all power and grace, all Don't fuck with me. Nike. Messenger of the gods and goddesses. In pale-blue marble. One foot touching as she lights on earth, bearing a message. The power of Winged Victory's form surged through me like lightning strikes.

Muscle legs with roots that stretched to the earth's core. Hips bruised and leathery. Power hips. Shoulder and arm muscles brawny too. I sucked down mountain air. Thin. Clean. Sharp. Lungs puffed. Ribs grew. Breasts rose. Heart banged through bones and skin. Blisters, scrapes, cuts, bug bites, skin dirt—forgotten. I blinked the Wyoming sky. Sky that pierced with its blueness, its big skyness. Sky that cradled the sunflower sun. I threw my arms wide and stretched to the blue, to the yellow, to the one cloud shaped like a crown. I could have eaten it.

Two weeks of steer-wrestling my bull of a pack. Two weeks of struggle and grit and I'm-not-fucking-giving-up. Tears too. I shed tubs of tears as I learned to wrangle my pack, snug straps, stumble, and push on no matter what.

Every night, after hiking 10 or more miles each day, after popping up our tent, making dinner, scrubbing dishes with pinecones, I'd slink away from the group in search of a crying spot. The first two weeks it was too much. All of it. My pack, the hiking, my blisters, my group that was all faster and stronger. You're only as fast as your slowest hiker, the instructors would remind us, and I felt angry eyes zeroed on me. The first week I wordlessly begged for a way out. A side door. Trap door. Any door I could conjure to slip through and slip out of the woods.

In the mornings, I'd be grateful for a cup of cowboy coffee (coffee grounds boiled on a mini stove) and remind myself: There is no quit in me. I'd put fresh moleskin on my blisters, pack up camp, strap on my backpack—that slowly, oh so slowly, morphed from monster to friend—and go.

I never got good (not even okay) at orienteering: navigating by compass and map. Dense woods, boulder fields, even ridge lines looked like giant repeating doodles on our folded-out, folded-up maps with their bent edges and shabby corners.

When we were split into groups of four and given a spot on the topographical map to meet in two days? I got lost with my group. We tripped off course and then snow snowed us in and we couldn't see, couldn't course correct. I tripped and crashed. Jammed and twisted my ankle. It plumped to double so I left my boot on in case it was broken. Miles from medical help, a boot can step up as a make-do cast.

As snow amped up and lightning cracked the sky, as panic filled our guts and mouths, we decided to pile the four of us in a two-person tent. We smelled it up with fear.

We're going to die out here, one guy said. One of the teens who raced through the woods like his pack was stuffed with clouds.

We're not, I said. Even though in my head it was all: *Fuck. Fuck. Fuck. We could die.* Even though I was picturing our local Tacoma Tribune headline: "Four NOLS Students Die in Snowstorm. One Family Sobs: 'We Begged Her not to Go.'"

The first night with the four of us noodled together, snow pelted the nylon tent as thunder crashed and lightning dazzled the sky. The time between rumble and spiked light was less than a second, so we knew it was close.

Fuck! we four yelled as Zeus's sky bolts lit the blue tent.

Shit! we yelled as we held each other close. Our sleeping bags a veneer between shaky bodies.

We're going to d—

We're not, I said, my voice steady even though my insides quivered. Not tonight.

That first night the four of us slept—when we slept—in a pile of whimpers. A pile of sleeping bags: navy, forest green, rust, maroon, all packed with bodies. Me with my fat ankle, sprained but not broken, angled away from the other three.

The next morning after hot chocolate and cold granola, after all eight eyes studied the lines and swirls like blown-up fingerprints on the topographical map, after all four voices said where we thought we were and where we slid or maybe vaulted off course, we sent two scouts to find the main group. I stayed behind with my throbbing ankle and my It's going to be okay words.

Our two scouts returned in the dark. Two. Not more. Not help.

Did we talk that night?

I mostly remember silence.

I mostly remember the throb of my heart in my ears.

That night I dreamed Aunt Jean—my aunt I'd always been close with who died my freshman year of college—walked through the snow to find me. She stood outside the tent, dressed in white jeans, a low-scoop tangerine blouse, and her white strappy sandals she loved.

Aunt Jean! I shouted in my dream.

You're going to be okay, she said as snow stuck to wisps of her auburn hair and her coral lipstick. You got stretch in you, Sugar. Always remember that.

The second morning I woke to hearing our names called, far away. I unwound myself from my sleeping bag, unzipped the tent and yelled, We're here! We're over here!

Even with all the struggle and swearing all the swears I knew, heart-mashing beauty trumped the hard parts that month in the woods. Mountains and sky and sun sliced the canopy, sliced the clouds. I slept under star blankets, the Milky Way splashed across the sky, waxing moon, waning moon, an entire moon cycle. Me, wrapped in the darkest dark I'd ever been in. I couldn't see my fingers even when I touched my face.

I learned to pitch a tent faster than my tentmate could return with water from the close by stream.

I learned to take care of my feet and fit blisters with dough-nut-shaped moleskin faster than my group could guzzle water on a break.

I learned to pee and poop in the woods.

Not care about a shower.

Stop smelling my pits because I was past onion, past earthy, past decay smell.

I learned to cook bread on a rock.

Make a splint out of tree limbs.

I learned to ask What now? instead of saying, I should have, like when I tripped and crashed in a boulder field, got stuck be-tween stones bigger than my VW Bug.

What now? When I fell off a zip-line crossing an icy river with my pack on.

What now? When a bear batted my sleeping bag and chewed holes in my sleeping pad while we were rock climbing, away from our campsite.

Every blister, every tear, every bruise and cut and mosquito bite:

Worth it.

Double worth it.

To straddle The Continental Divide. Boots in the dirt. Heart wrapped in sky. To feel my wingbones break skin.

It's me! I shouted at the mountains and trees and endless sky. My legs strong to the earth. Shoulders back. Breasts out. I leaned in. All power and grace. Plus wings. Iridescent feathers. Steel strong feathers. Nike wings.

I made it!

I was every explorer who'd ever reached the summit. Who'd beamed with giddy. I etched this moment in the bone of memory. This victory would hold me when I needed the reminder I was made of Earth, Air, Fire, and Water. Whenever I needed to remember:

I can do anything. Any. Damn. Thing.

Before

Nothing ever dies, Kent said on one of our long drives in the Getting to Know You and I'm Mad about You stage. A rainbow in the distance, spearing the cliff and beach. Windows down. My tanned arm in the air stream, hand rolling in waves against the rush of cool ocean air, tangy on skin.

You know that, right? he said.

What? I lifted my sunglasses and turned toward him.

Nothing dies. Energy's not lost. It transforms.

All right, I said, and thought about high school physics and my favorite teacher Mr. Eastly with his plaid shirts and wire-rimmed glasses. I wished I'd paid more attention in high school now that I was in love with a physicist.

Matter isn't broken, he said to the hum of the ocean just out the window, staring through the windshield at the dandelion sun.

Sometimes alive-him would pinch his arm with, See this? It's packaging. This body, all muscle and bones, organs and skin. Really, we're all energy walking around in a meat body. And whatever happens to this? he'd say, tapping his chest, half-shrugging, his voice a question. Energy's never lost. It becomes something else.

After

Kent's ashes were stored in a cardboard box. Puzzle-sized box: smooth, white, sturdy. Of course I thought of a puzzle box, too easy of a metaphor, both of us unpuzzled then. Him in the night sky. Me in a jumble of mystery shapes.

Cardboard box with half his ashes. The other half in the ground sealed with a bronze plaque with his name and birth and death dates. Buried near my grandparents and uncle. Up the hill from where my parents will be buried. My dead family at Mountain View Cemetery, Mount Rainier always in the backdrop.

In the early death decisions when I was a human popsicle with no voice, splitting his ashes felt like a horrid compromise—like the only compromise.

His parents wanted a full—not burned—body burial. All of their son in the ground.

Please don't cremate him, they said.

It's what he wanted.

It's not, they said, even though I knew it was.

It's not right.

Please don't, they pleaded through sheets of tears.

The worst thing had happened: their beloved son died. I couldn't pile worst on worst, even though I was adamant about cremation.

They changed their teary ask to, At least bury him, when I told them Kent wanted his ashes scattered in the mountains. Please bury his ashes so we can visit him, they said, wringing hands, mine and theirs. Please.

So I compromised. Middle-me in the swirl of middle ground searching for middle. I buried half of him.

I tucked the white cardboard box in the bottom of my daypack. Sturdy cardboard. Corrugated. About 5x7x3 inches. The weight of him. The not-weight. The heft of half a body.

I added water, string cheese and grapes, baby wipes, and a spare diaper to my pack. New essentials to my 10 essentials. I tucked a favorite heart-shaped beach rock in a side pocket. I zipped, snapped, and strapped, like so many packs before. This pack was easy. Just bones and memories.

The notness of him.

Can I carry that for you? Scot asked, chin tipped down, sea-blue eyes tipped up. I mean, only if you want me to. I sure understand if you don't.

I swallowed hard. My tongue fat and sandpapery.

I shook my head, No.

I started to say it was weird enough to have him there, but words wouldn't come. I wiggled my tongue in my clamped mouth.

I got it, I said. I heard my own echo. My words clanged around in the hollow of my bones.

Before we shut and locked my steel-blue Taurus wagon, Scot raised a can of Cherry Coke I'd brought to the mountain.

Do you want to take this? he asked, his voice on soft. Or is it for after?

I'd told him how Kent loved Cherry Coke. I'd told him how drinking a Cherry Coke, how raising a Cherry Coke to Kent on birthdays and other celebration days was one way I honored my dead husband. I had snapped one open on the drive to Mount Rainier. Swallowed a tiny mouthful of sweet Coke bubbles while I did my best to tell Scot what I needed.

Can you be with me and not be with me? I asked, while the tingle of Coke bubbles lingered between my words. I don't even know what that means, I added.

The torn-ness in my chest. I'd said No to everyone else who asked if they could come when I scattered Kent's ashes.

This is just for me, I'd said to my sisters, my parents, Kent's sister, friends. I said it to Kent's best friend, Ron, another mountain man, who went quiet on the phone, cleared his throat, and told me he understood.

Just for me.

And Jake.

However you need me to be there, I'll be there, Scot said while we wound the freeway, the highway, the side of the mountain, while I sipped a sip of that sugary Coke extra-sweetness, while bubbles bubbled up my nose.

Mount Rainier. The traditional land of the Cowlitz, Muckleshoot, Nisqually, Puyallup, Squaxin Island, and Yakima tribes. Mount Rainier. Majestic. Massive. Looming in light and shadow. Mountain of rock and trees and snow and ice. Mountain speared electric-blue sky. A mountain with a saddle, sized for a giant. Groomed trails. No trails. Flint-grey rock. Grass dotted with meadow flowers in summer. Clusters of Douglas fir, western red cedar, and western hemlock. Mountain birds. Northwest spotted owls lived here too even though I'd never seen one. A Cowlitz legend tells of a time Mount Rainier argued with his two wives, Mount Saint Helens and Mount Adams. Mount Saint Helens erupted in jealousy, knocking the head off Mount Rainier. When Mom was a girl, her two older brothers teased her, the way brothers will, calling her Little Mount Rainier on Wheels. When I was a girl, I spent my girlhood in the shadow of this mountain with its dip where I imagined a head.

Paradise Lodge squatted straight ahead of us, tucked into the mountain, crafted of old timber and stone: warm and inviting, picturesque. Carloads of people visited the lodge year-round and soaked in the expansive view, the lung-scrubbing air, the goodness.

Ready? I asked Jake and Scot. I asked myself.

Ready Mama! Jake half-shouted and wrapped his arms around my thighs.

The parking lot was jammed with cars and trucks and mini vans that sunny October Saturday. Soft sun: the taste of fall—apples, cinnamon, slowing down—and crunchy leaves in crimson, butterscotch, and pumpkin colors. A jagged wind pushed in stops and starts. Families and not-families milled around the bathrooms and benches. Around the map with the smudged "You are Here" spot worn to the bone.

I eyed the map. Searched memory for which direction I'd last gone with Kent. Memory. A fickle partner. Where was it when I needed it?

I adjusted the pack with my half-husband inside.

We'll hike a little and when you get tired, I'll carry you. Okay? Okay! Jake said, squinting up at me.

Jake grabbed my hand with: Let's go, Mama! He stomped his mini hiking boots with their waffle soles. He stretched his other hand to Scot.

My arms flared in goosebumps at my boy so easily reaching for Scot.

October sun sunned our crowns, warmed our three heads of walnut-colored hair, spotlighted the auburn underglow in Jake's hair, in mine. Sun threw leggy shadows behind us. The three of us, hand in hand in hand, shadow shaped like the mountain with its tall/short/tall saddle dip.

Mama? Jake asked in his way. In all the ways he used Mama as joy, uncertainty, fear, safety, happy.

I'm okay, Bud, I said, soft as dandelion seed.

I am.

After

We hiked a path that curved and climbed, then leveled and fanned to a wide meadow with brown grass, splashes of late season white and yellow meadow flowers, seed pods, a cluster of short evergreens. A bird shadow swooshed on the ground in front of us, its wings wide in glide. Me leading. Jake in my arms, at my side, on Scot's shoulders. Kent in a box at the dip of my spine. The all of everything and nothing wadded up.

The path split. My internal compass spiraled like when I got lost in the snowstorm in the Wyoming mountains. Inner compass said Go right. So I almost went left. But my gut or the wind or something bigger said, Trust yourself.

Up? Jake asked and toddled toward me with his hands above his head.

Want me to carry him? Scot asked.

In a bit, I said, reminding myself to not say No on autopilot, reminding myself that it was good to widen our circle, to be a three with this man who loved us, who still moved with caution.

Come here, Jakester. I swung him up on my hip.

The breeze pushed the clouds away from the sun. It was close to three o'clock and our slanted shadow imitated some stretched-out pack animal.

A good mountaineer slows but doesn't stop. Words I heard on repeat the 30 days I backpacked. I slowed. Slowed more. Kept going.

Jake fingered the hair at the nape of my neck like he did when he was sleepy. He tented his forehead with mine.

I know it's nap time, I whispered, and he dropped his head on my shoulder, slumped into the curve of my neck, the sink above my collarbone.

We'll carry you all the way down, I promised. You can sleep in the car.

He sagged deeper, heavier. I slid him to my chest, wished I'd brought the backpack for carrying him rather than the backpack for carrying Kent. My heart boomed between my front load and back load. Between my After life and Before life.

You two all right? Scot asked.

Me all sweaty and breathing hard.

Jake doubled in weight. I tightened my grip. Kent's wedding ring, that I'd put back on a chain around my neck that morning, pressed my ribs and dug a circle into skin. All my I-can-do-it-myselfness pulsed through me as I huffed and held my boy. Then this thought: Let Scot help.

Will you take him?

Of course, he said, arms wide.

Over the next knoll, I spotted a small clearing to the left, with an alpine garden—flowers, granite rocks—protected by trees. No one above. No one behind. And a log.

Here, I said, and my truth pendulum pinged. It's perfect.

As soon as Jake saw the log he slid from Scot's hold and flung himself across it.

Water? I offered and pulled out the water bottle.

He stretched his little hands, fingers spread. Two starfish.

I have string cheese too and grapes, I told him.

And a heavy/not heavy white cardboard box.

Was it selfish to be here, just with Jake and Scot? Maybe. Probably. Absolutely. Kent's family lost a son, brother, uncle. My family lost a son-in-law, brother-in-law. Friends lost a gravity friend and their orbits wobbled. Their heartaches weren't lost on me. And yet, there I was. Without them.

This part is for me. And Jake.

This pull to spread Kent's ashes with only Kent. Me. And our son who was still dabbling in the stars when Kent told me if he died first, scatter his ashes in the mountains.

It's where I belong, he said back then. It's home.

I couldn't have imagined there'd be Scot too when I packed Kent home. This tender man with his own father loss, a loss that tuned him to ours while my grief opened conversations he hadn't had, bringing him a kind of healing too. He stepped off the path to the hard packed dirt. Outside the circle of Jake and me.

I fished a rumpled paper from my front pocket, extra rumpled from me sweating.

I don't know how I'm supposed to do this, I said, and my throat shrank. The words I'd scratched out the night before blurred as tears gathered at the shores of me.

I opened the flap of the box. A plastic bag sealed with a red twist tie.

Kent's ashes. Grey like his hair. Flecks of white bones. Bone shards. Some big as my pinky fingernail. My You Can't Live Your Life in a Box husband. Boxed. Half of him anyway.

I dipped my fingers in the smooth, gritty, dusty, silky, course, ashy, bony, solid, formless ash. Like nothing I'd felt before. Like everything I'd felt before.

I'd said goodbye in so many ways on so many days. Goodbye to the warmth of him in bed and to his morning singing. Goodbye to him dancing me around the kitchen, hiking in the mountains, skiing with his coat flapping. Goodbye to his smell, his skin, his body tendrilled with mine. Goodbye to his laugh that spiked my joy meter. His wonder. His endless curiosity. He loved me pure like no one had.

But there was always more.

Grief is days and nights and not-days and not-nights of goodbye.

On repeat.

I wanted to believe enough goodbyes would get me to closure. And yet. Closure was bullshit. Something to say in a grief footnote. You don't close grief. It doesn't shrink. You grow yourself instead.

I clenched my words in one hand and a handful of Kent in the other.

What did I want?

Readiness. To at least be in the same room with ready. Ever since Kent died, I'd been bushwhacking through grief's forest, without a map or compass or machete. Ready felt galaxies away.

What did ready even mean?

I shoved the paper back in my pocket. I knew what to say.

I love you, Kent.

I'll always love you.

A fistful of Kent by my side. Unfisted. His ashes floated to the rocky ground. Tears tracked down my cheeks in those tear grooves that had faded some, that would never fully fade.

Jake belly-flopped on the log. Feet on one side. Hands stretched on the other.

Thank you for our beautiful boy, I said and smiled at Jake. This boy. Little boy yumminess. Draped on the weathered log.

I'll always be grateful for Jake-O, I said to the ice-blue sky. Fingers dipped back in the bag. I worried ashes between my fingers. Cupped a bigger handful. Silky. Silty. Smooth ash. Gravelly. Flecks of bone. Bone that'd been crushed in a bone crusher (the final step for cremated bodies) since bones don't burn.

I'll always love you, I said, tossing Kent to my side in an arc. This rainbow of my dead husband.

Two fistfuls. Gritty ashes. Velvety and coarse.

Gawd I miss you, I said.

Fat tears. Twist in my belly. Fire in my ears.

I unfurled my fists and his ashes slipped through, slow. Hourglass sand.

Jake found a stick. Flopped back on the log. Straddled it. Rode it. Used the stick like a riding crop. He clucked at his horse log: Go, go!

I wiped tears with the back of my hand and cupped more ashes.

I know you're not here, I said. Hoarse words. My throat thick with longing.

You're not this body. Not what's left of it, I said.

I flung ashes in a circle.

You are everywhere and nowhere.

But you're always here, I said, hand circling my heart.

Tears turned on high. I hadn't cried that hard for months. Yet here I was. Thunder tears. Conjuring mountain husband tears. I wanted creation myth. Tears from the well of me, the dark of me, to mix with ashes, form ash husband like those old stories of people formed from clay, from snow, from ice.

I wanted.

But the magic of my tears was something different.

I breathed to the bottom of my lungs. That wet in-and-out place where hope rested and bloomed. I soaked in the mountain-blue sky, the forest-green trees, the scorched-brown grass. The massive mountain in front of me. Mount Rainier. Always in my backdrop. Girlhood first. Then I fell in love with Kent hiking here. Married him close by at a lake and a meadow. Three-and-a-half years later he died on a mountain road. Then I spread his ashes near a tree on the mountain. My mountain man. Home.

Jake glanced my way and blinked. He buzzed his lips.

I love you, Bud, I said. With all of me.

Jake loves Mama! he said and kicked the log with his waffle stompers, kicked it how he'd seen his aunties ride horses, how I rode as a girl, how I last rode when I was pregnant with him, how his sister/my daughter (still a wish beyond wishing stars) would ride one day.

The box with its clear plastic liner was three-quarters empty, one-quarter full. I'd said what I wanted to say.

Now what?

Do I keep spreading? Take Kent home?

I scooped the end of his ashes and brought the gritty silkiness close to my nose to breathe him in. The smell of ash. Dirt. Earth. Human.

I sneezed.

Reader, I sneezed.

And that made me snort-laugh. I swear I could hear Kent's giant belly laugh too.

I spread the rest close to the tree. Some under so the tree could shade them. Some farther out so the sun could warm them. I spread him to leave a map. Then I plucked a heart-shaped rock from the pack—a favorite find from a California beach with a pinkish vein bisecting the heart— traced the vein with my thumb and tucked it under the tree too.

I gripped that empty cardboard box and knew my first-love husband was all around. That he did what he'd set out to do. And it was enough.

I dusted my hands. Licked my fingers.

Then scooped Jake. Nuzzled him. Forehead to forehead. This tent of us. Breathed him in: little boy dustiness and deliciousness. He flung his arms around my neck. Fingered my neck hairs with his tiny hands. His heart beat against mine and here was my life. Me. Alive. With my beautiful son.

I peered over Jake's shoulder at Scot. He stroked his beard and half-smiled. This beloved man who held my heart. Who dabbed more gold into the kintsugi of me. Who was patient and kind. Who loved us from afar. Who loved us up close.

Life was fat with possibilities.

After

So he's not a toad? Liz asked at group time, grinning at me. I—fast—swallowed the coffee in my mouth to keep from spitting it out in a laugh.

So not a toad, I said. I'd told them about spreading Kent's ashes. I'd told my widow posse how Scot spread a web of kindness. How he was able to be with me without saying the kinds of things people say in an effort to comfort. I told them how he offered a Cherry Coke he'd carried undercover. When I saw my ashy fingerprints—Kent's ashes, my whorls—on the back of Jake's jacket, when I felt I'd done what I came to do and it was good, Scot fished out the Coke, raised it toward me in a question: Now?

I feel so lucky, I said, pushing at my tears with my middle knuckle. The tears I cried at overwhelm. Not happy. Not sad. Not the bottomless tears of grief. More like relief. Like the little fizz splash sound Coke makes when you click open a can.

I never thought I'd feel lucky again, I said, and that pool of wet that rode at the top of my ribs, at the meeting spot of my collarbones, sloshed tears up my throat, past the root of my tongue.

I'm so glad I was wrong, I went. So glad sorrow doesn't have to wipe out joy.

After

My college-and-beyond friend Debra visited from Los Angeles a few months after Scot moved his clothes and shoes and bass guitars and upright bass and Ingeborg—his I–only-love-Scot cat—into my home. After I made room in my closet and the chambers of my heart. The winter before we married.

When Kent and I married, Debra was a bridesmaid with my sisters. Three women I loved like sky. Three women all summer floral in pastel pink, robin-egg blue, and faded mint-green Laura Ashley dresses they never wore again. Later, Debra parked on the phone for hours while I sobbed in my hardest grief. She flew to meet Jake when he was weeks new. My true blonde blue-eyed heartline friend with a chipmunk laugh.

Stars out. Crescent moon cresting. Debra and I were finishing up glasses of merlot and laughing in the warm of my family room with a fire snapping in the fireplace. Jake and Scot upstairs sleeping. Their dreams in the moon.

Remember that time you went on that blind date our freshmen year? Debra said.

In the borrowed red dress and stilettos?

And the short guy showed up? She laughed a blast of laugh, one hand pressed to her bellybutton.

But I couldn't ditch the shoes, I said, remembering my surprise to meet this guy, short as me, shorter than me in heels. The ah-ha moment: You set me up because I'm 5'2" and now I'm taller than him in heels and oh shit I blew that one and oh well I can't ditch the shoes or I'd walk on the sexy sparkle dress that's not mine.

I loved that dress, I said, wiping tears from the corners of my eyes.

What about the guy?

I don't even remember his name. But that dress. All sparkly and tight and low-cut. Like nothing I'd worn before.

Oh, we had fun getting you ready.

Yeah, I nodded.

Debra's roommate had owned the sexy dress and fuck-me shoes. Together my friends styled my hair and made my eyes smoky, my lips Coca-Cola red, since makeup to me equaled ponytail holders and Bonne Bell clear lip gloss.

What we didn't know then.

We took long sips of wine.

I stared straight in Debra's lake-blue eyes.

Thank you for sticking with me, I said, my voice wispy at the end. I choked a little on *sticking with me.*

Of course, she said and waved me off.

Not everyone stuck with me.

I leaked a long, slow breath. Then a chuckle. This long sigh, a leak in a bike tire. Like a Scot sigh. Scot. Who I joked was the complex sigher.

I love seeing you happy again.

Thank you, I said even though Thank you felt puny.

In the morning, snow blanketed my neighborhood. Puget Sound, salt water that points to the ocean, so blue against winter white. Rhododendrons and naked maples and firs all glistened in the snow sparkle. Crystals formed in the freeze. Everything layered in marshmallow crème as if the snow fairies frosted the world while we slept.

It was magical from the warm of home.

But.

This beautiful snow. It terrified me. The wet and ice of it. Add northwest snow drivers, unskilled risk takers.

I wanted everyone to stay in. Stay safe.

Can you stay? I asked Debra as soon as she woke to the smell of coffee.

I have to go, she said. I gotta be back at work.

Scot was in the kitchen too. He'd stayed to drive her to the airport when he woke to twinkle snow and didn't want her to risk a cab.

Could she and Scot see my heart blasting outside of my body? Could they see the shimmer of me? The me that exploded and swirled around the room? Shapeshifted from body-me to bodiless-me. Particles of fear in mini cyclones.

It'll be okay, Scot said, his hands finding mine. You know I'll be careful.

Please stay, I pleaded, my voice husky and low. It's too risky.

All the ways I'd learned to calm myself with breath and visualizing and loving words. All of it. Gone.

I can't miss my flight, she said, her eyes lasered on Scot, her eyes full of *Please explain it to her.*

Scot's cocoon of arms circled my icy body. His breath. His words in my scalp.

I'll be careful. I know you're scared, he whispered. But I have to take her. We can't stay shut in.

And I heard Kent loud, as if he was standing in the same room: You can't live your life in a box.

But what if I want to? I asked back, wordlessly.

What if a box would have kept you alive?

Nah, Kent said. Thirty-six years was right for me this time. This life. Thirty-six years. Five of them with you. Lucky me.

I cradled Scot's hand. His hands. Not much bigger than mine. His beautiful hands with their finger callouses from playing the bass. From plucking thick strings that vibrated sound. Deep like whale song. Deep like the earth's heartbeat.

You're a bass player? I said on our first date when he showed up in his Honda station wagon and I was surprised a single guy drove a wagon. I remembered him joking that he'd be a piccolo player in his next life. Something he could carry in his hip pocket.

I kissed the back of his hand. Warm and smooth with veins rivering straight to his bass heart. His hands that held me. That held Jake. Hands that plucked his upright bass and electric bass too. His upright bass with its sexy curves. The size and shape so like the female body. Female sound too when I thought of women's voices holding the world.

I love that you kiss my hand, he said the first time, the second time, the almost every time I did it.

No one's done that before, he said.

Steadying myself in the kitchen that winter day with Scot and Debra, while she said she needed to catch her flight home and he said he needed to drive her to the airport, and it was going to be okay while I blinked and blinked to concentrate to hear It's going to be okay and not push it away, not hear it like I was under water.

I gulped hard around the pebbles in my throat feeling and pressed my body into Scot's. I tentacled my body to his.

If this were the last time I'd hold Scot, what would I say?

It felt like I got a redo—impossible, but here it was. I could say to Scot what I longed to have said to Kent.

I love you.

The same words I said to Kent.

I love you.

All three words. I. Love. You. Not the quick Love You or even quicker Luv Ya.

The same last words I said to my stepdad years later before he died.

I love you.

The same last words I said to my dad more years later before he died.

I love you.

Because.

Love.

It's what I have to give.

After

The cave smelled wet in a wet I hadn't smelled before. Dank and salty. The air thick and moist. I swallowed and earth lingered on my tongue—metal, mineral, penny, steel wool.

I didn't think I could leave little Jake-O, but the tug to go to New Zealand had beaten fear. The first time for Scot and Me Time. When I told my sisters we were going, they both said, Of course you are. You have to find out if you like the guy.

Two weeks. Seven-thousand miles from Jake. My boy I'd never spent a night away from. I landed in New Zealand with mama panic, stomach squiggling like I'd swallowed a puddle of pollywogs. Plane wheels skimmed the Auckland runway and I announced: I'm catching the next plane back.

Can we stay one day? Sleep? Then decide? Scot asked, holding my hand. Exactly what I needed.

Careful there, the tour guide cautioned, as a middle-aged woman in butter-yellow and lizard-green plaid Bermuda shorts wobbled, sunglasses snug on her hot-pink visor. One foot in the boat. One on the dock in the cave. The guide's offered hand steadied her, steadied the boat—long and narrow like a gondola.

The boat dipped side to side as we tourists settled on the plank seats. Two people per row. Me, almost in Scot's lap.

First, we'll go into the Glowworm Caves, the guide told the 10 of us. Then we'll go in the Cathedral.

The Waitomo Glowworm Caves, two hours south of Auckland.

Do you want to see the Glowworm Caves? Scot had asked when we were planning our trip from the bigness of my family room.

Sure, I said. I mean, we have to see it, right?

Not if it makes you uncomfortable, he said. It is a cave.

He was right. Caves and claustrophobia—a pulse in my ears just putting those words in the same sentence. But I wanted to see all those tiny glowworms, like the cosmos at night, endless glitter light.

Let's go, I said. Let's.

Waitomo is a Maori word, the college-aged guide in safari khakis told us as he guided the boat with a pole, gondola-style. *Wai* means water and *tomo* is entrance or hole. So it translates as a stream that flows in a hole in the ground.

We floated deeper and deeper in the dark cave.

With each plant of the guide's stick, water licked the boat.

The cool of underground.

You okay? Scot asked, gripping my slimy hand.

With each lift and dip of the pole, my breathing thinned.

I got you, he said, pulling me closer.

I breathed in hard. Out hard.

Then I looked up.

The ceiling pulsed in glowworms: thousands of tiny lights. Miniature flashlights. Glow-in-the-dark stars splashed above like the night sky in the country where you can peer into the Milky Way. But here, we were up close. A hundred nights of fireflies all squished into one.

I was so full of wonder, I forgot to be scared.

The mini lights multiplied, reflected in the water. This galaxy of lights above and below. Us drifting in the constellations. It was the closest thing I could imagine to being in space.

Kent would have loved this, I whispered.

I remembered him saying how if space flight opened up to everybody, he'd go. We'd mortgage the house, sell it, hawk body and body to go, he said. Even if it's one way. Will you go with me? Please say you will.

If it's one way, can we be older? I asked, and Kent just winked and laughed.

I'm sure he would have, Scot said, without missing a beat. I wish he'd seen it too.

Goosebumps mushroomed—pop—as though they'd been right at the surface of my skin. Here was my truth: I loved two men to the bone of me. The one swimming and cartwheeling in the cosmos, holding the universe together. The tender openhearted one at my side. I felt a new story stitching in all the twinkle lights. My heart boomed like it was too big for my chest, like it was just right.

After

Tenderhearted. Surehearted. Bravehearted. Heartsong. Heart as muscle. Honey soaked. Four chambers: left ventricle, right ventricle, left atrium, right atrium. Fifth chamber gushing and pumping. What gets held in the fifth? More love, beauty, grace. More of what makes me, me: what makes you, you.

Boom, boom, swish heart. Heart sac. Heart holes. Stitched with lightning. Stitched with love. Heart murmur as echo, wet whisper. Heart. Carmine conductor. Slippery engine. Underscore. Beat. Bass cleft. Bass line. Bass player. Bass man.

Of course I picked you when I thought my heart was broken. After Kent died on an icy road. After Jake swam out of me and to me. After you slipped into my life tasting like jazz and starlight. Honey man. Bass man. Holding the beat. Almost deaf in your right ear from standing by drummers since you were 13. When you put away your cello and concert clothes and strummed the bass. Started serenading and seducing me from miles and years away though neither of us knew it yet.

The beat of you. Ground. Beat. Heart. Beat. Bass line. Glue. Granite. Rock. The rhythm of you. Horsehair bow. Four strings. Four chambers. A fifth growing. Muscle heart. Beating. Thrumming. In the quiet of me. In the voice of me. You have my heart. You are my heart. Here's my heart.

After

Past the twinkling glowworm lights, on the other end of the dark, was a lit part of the cave. All 11 of us from the boat, single file, clomped along a path worn smooth by thousands of feet.

Mind your head, the tour guide cautioned.

Scot ducked deeper than me to keep from smacking into a stalagmite. Or was it stalactite? One growing up. The other down. I could never keep it straight.

You okay? he asked, pulling me close.

You did great on the boat, he whispered. You'll let me know?

Keep holding my hand, I said and squeezed his. If I concentrated on his back rather than the fact that I was underground, in a cave, walls on all sides of me, my skin itching from the inside out, I had a better chance of not panicking.

It's beautiful if you can look, he said.

I'd peek at the ceiling with its limestone crystals, glance at the sand-colored walls, this underground desert, then straight back to

Scot's faded yellow polo shirt. My tongue turned sticky. My silent mantra: I'm okay. I'm okay. Just breathe. Just breathe.

Stay on the path, the guide reminded us again, his flashlight glinting off the walls, making long shadows that inked to black when he moved the beam.

Follow me.

We threaded our way through the stalagmites/stalactites, resisting the urge to touch them. Just when panic started walking louder, we reached the end where the cave was bright with lights, with tall walls the color of sandstone. Column walls looked carved like organ pipes. Standing in that natural cathedral I could feel the earth's heartbeat. The walls breathing. The ground pulsing.

This is a special place, the guide started.

Wide-eyed, I felt all my girl-wonder. I wanted to cartwheel and shout. I wanted to freeze. I wanted to soak it all in, make a memory deep in my bones. Covered in goosebumps that bloomed from my bends (elbows, neck, knees) out. It was more than the cold from being underground. A reverence, a peacefulness, a sacredness. It felt holy.

My fears quieted in the wonder of it all.

It's called the Cathedral, the guide went on.

I bet the acoustics are great in here, Scot said, my amazing bass playing perfect-pitch love.

They are, the guide said. Some pretty famous people have sung in here.

It's stunning, was all I managed to squeak out, soaking in the cave, so beautifully sculpted by nature. The shades of sand with flecks of bronze and tan, with a shimmer of burnt sienna. The sound of water gently lapping behind us.

Scot at my side. This man. This second chance at happiness when I thought all my happy was used up. He hugged me from behind. His heart on the back of my heart. The thump thump of him. The scent of him—like water.

I love you, he whispered in my left ear, the one closest to my heart.

We were in our own little bubble. Then one of us said: Let's get married here. Now.

Then the other said, Yes, Let's get married here. Today.

Oh, the guide said. People get married here. Isn't it a beautiful spot?

It's gorgeous, I said, slow, words finding their way back to me. Those columns smacked me with their beauty.

We could—

We could.

I tingled all over. I could see it: just the two of us with strangers for witnesses. The two of us committing to each other in this beautiful church cave. No wedding dress. No fuss. Pledging my love to this love of a man.

Okay, I said. I love it.

Let's.

We almost did. Almost.

I don't remember which one of us was first to say, Jake needs to be with us. And our families. We wanted them inside our joy.

Married over 33 years now, sometimes one of us will say: Remember when we almost got married in the cave in New Zealand? And the other usually sighs. We almost did. In that magic spot. We almost. Without a license. We almost. Without an officiate. We almost.

That early bliss bubble, we carried it in our hearts. Past the night sky of glowworms, in that most stunning cathedral of stone, we pledged our love: partners, lovers, friends, sidekicks, heart-throbs, glue, ground, heart.

I do.

And I do.

And I do.

After

Polka dot lights splashed the hospital floor. Light orbs with fuzzy edges flitted like fairy lights under the window under the heat register under our shoes. Gossamer light layered with lingering Pine-Sol, lingering life.

Me at 36. Huddled with family around Nana's hospital bed. The Pease clan. Nana's legacy. Her two sons. Three daughters-in-law. Nine grandchildren. Grandchildren spouses. No great grand-kids here even though she had 10.

If people die the way they live, and I'm pretty sure they do, Nana was in her element. Family.

Nana. Once stout and strong grandmother, now maybe one-hundred pounds. All bones and loose skin and coiled back. If she could roll, expose her spine, I could count her vertebrae without touching her. Tracks just under skin. Life spine: girl, daughter, student, wife, mother, teacher, grandmother, great-grandmother. Fried chicken cooking queen. Homemade potato roll master. Plant grower. Lover of order. Of Jesus and church and organ music. Of pearls and rhinestones. Of books and Geritol and Lawrence Welk. Loved her boys fierce, her grandkids fiercer.

Silver hair, thick and curly. Cut close in a Senior #2 cut. Her mouth a sour cavity without dentures. A morphine drip bruised up her skim-milk blue skin. Her strength and steel a memory. Her Remember I'm Your Victorian Grandmother speech (when I'd swear or smoke or speak my truth, she'd say those words slow and pat her curly curls.) Gone. Motionless as dead. No muscle holding. No tense. Melty. Bony. Squishy grandma. This woman who always held tight. Now letting go.

It's okay, Mom, Dad said, rubbing the top of her bony hand, her onion paper skin. It's okay for you to die.

She didn't blink or twitch as he said these words. I counted the seconds between her breaths. Ten. Twenty. Thirty. Then she'd suck in a long jagged breath through her cave mouth. More gasp than breath, shallow with hard edges. Last breaths in gasps, like the dying are surprised.

Dad said more words.

We love you, he said, tears leading off the point of his nose. It's okay for you to go.

His words.

Soft.

Low.

I leaned in to hear the vowels of his love words.

Morphine dripped.

Cart squeaked in the hall.

My dad who choked on feelings. My normally pressed and polished dad here at the hospital, unshaven, unshowered. Perched on the metal folding chair since the day before.

I have to stay, he said when any of us suggested he take a break. I have to.

We love you, Mom, he whispered. It's okay for you to die.

My arm hairs stood straight up. Death's breath on my skin.

I never loved my dad more than I loved him in this moment.

When her last breath was her last. When no more air pumped lungs. When her 86-year-old heart stopped. This dying all tumbled up with all of us living. The gift of being with Nana when she left her body, when I felt her swirl above us, watching her beloveds hold her cooling hands through a veil of tears. While it couldn't balance out my trauma over Kent's sudden, violent death, it eased my heart, let me witness another way to leave your body. The peace of a good death. The beauty of it.

Before and After

ow to Marry Two Husbands

Squint at the sun through the double French doors, the threshold from here to next. Scot already on your friends' deck, waiting for bride-you to join him, to say I do. I do. Right after you say, Here's my heart. It's a little bruised, and here it is.

Squint and see your first wedding. That steamy August day with seersucker-blue sky and canary-yellow sun. With cotton candy clouds in puzzle pieces. With family and friends. By a lake where peacocks fan iridescent lapis and jade feathers, where a trumpeting swan spreads its wings when Kent says I do, when he wraps you in a hug, bends you back, and kisses you.
You say I do. Right after you say, Here's my heart.

Before you stepped into the heat to marry your first-love husband, you half-spun in the full-length mirror one more time. You in your cloud-white, strapless, watermark taffeta dress, ankle length even though it was 1983 and bridal dresses were extra, like all of fashion was extra. You felt lost in the poofy dresses at the bridal stores with their trains, with their endless layers of puff and tulle. It was like playing dress-up, but you were miles from being the girl who danced around the house in stick-out crinoline slips pretending they were tutus.

That sticky August day when your dad hugged you in the bride's dressing room, your hummingbird heart trilling so fast, he leaned in with minty breath and asked, voice on low, Do you want a Valium?

You pulled back and eyed your dad. His soft face, acorn-colored eyes framed by rectangular wire-rim glasses, not the horned-rimmed glasses from your girl years.

No, you said to your dad's Valium question. I want to feel it all.

Half?

Six years later your heart stung at the memory. Stung since your mom and stepdad weren't there the first time you married. Your mom whose credo, I'll never see or speak to your father again, rang louder than your first wedding day.

Those were the facts. Who was there and who wasn't. Your beautiful sisters. Your older sis with her almond eyes and chestnut hair. Your younger sis who you've called Snow White with raven hair, fair skin, and cherry-red lipstick. Kent's parents and sister and her family. A web of friends. All grinning, witnessing.

Six years later on a sun-soaked July day, Scot and his sister sang a duet out on the deck of your dear friends' home overlooking Puget Sound—a finger of water that points to the ocean. Deep-blue water. Aquamarine sky. The in-between of water and sky on the horizon. The flood of northwest green in their yard: emerald grass, maple trees dressed in lizard green, hostas with their forest green edged in white, leaves sculpted like elongated hearts.

You not in white taffeta. You in a black suit (skirt, not slacks) trimmed in white on the sleeves, white framing your collarbones, white setting off your rust-red lips.

I can wear it again, you told Scot, holding up the new black suit when you bought it the month before. I look good in black, you said. Are you okay with me wearing black?

You added a bride's mini hat with a mini veil, white lacey fishnets and white heels. Bride white bookending the black suit.

Widow bride. You couldn't see it then. You couldn't admit how you wore grief on your skin. How you were hoping grief would shrink to past tense, to shrank, as you stepped back into happy. Of course you wore black.

On the cusp of family: two to three. Cusp: from the Latin *cupis*, or point. Transition. Your swollen heart pointing the way from here to there.

Your beautiful toddler boy in one hand, with his dimple smile and handful of curls, with his hazel eyes, with his bounce in his sailor suit and saddle shoes. Your other hand sweating around stargazer lilies with their streaks of hot pink.

Your stampeding heart overflowed love and bliss and scared too. Room for all of it. All the feelings that filled and emptied the tide of your oceanic heart. Your fifth chamber, once micro as an orchid seed, now sister-sized to the other four chambers. Your muscle heart you thought was broken and it never was. Through the darkest dark, it beat and beat, the metronome of you, anchoring you in its boom, swish.

You poked your head outside to where your almost second husband and his sister sang a love duet. There was your family: sisters and parents. Your mom and stepdad (I feel like I have a second chance, your mom said.) Your dad. Maybe with a Valium in his pocket seam and he didn't offer it.

Just before you stepped through the French doors to Scot and the love circle of family, tiny black dots floated across your view. Some solid. Some outlined. The same tiny floating circles you'd seen all your life when your heart feels a truth.

Then. I love you, Kent whispered up close. The tickle of his not mustache on your pearl earring.

I'll always love you, he said, soft.

Goosebumps wrapped your arms. Tears swamped your throat. Wet your cheeks.

I love you too, you said, out loud. Your heart crumbled a little.

Did you have doubts?

You did.

Doubts born of loss, of fear, of *What if it happens again?* Doubts of your own demons that had nothing to do with Scot. Ugly doubts of whether you were good enough, whether you deserved all this happiness.

Now go, Kent said.

It's time.

A mini cyclone of light scooted across the hardwood floor, out the open doors, back to the sun.

What's that? Jake asked, pointing at the tumbleweed of light.

It's love, you said.

Pretty!

So beautiful, you said, wiping your slick face.

Like Mama.

You scooped him in one swoop. Up in your arms. Forehead to forehead. Skin to skin. This upside-down *V* you'd made since he was born.

Scot and his sister finished singing "Always." And you didn't make this up: birds sang. A hummingbird with its emerald-green bowtie zipped up to your chest, hovered, and shot away.

Let's go, Jake said, wiggling out of your arms with all his two-year-old joy. His hand in yours. Yours in his. You stepped from the cool of the house into the bumblebee sun.

After

I always wanted to see Mount St. Helens, said Kent's sister Sherry, from the backseat of our white Volvo 240 wagon Scot had bought me before we were married. My alive husband and me up front. My dead husband's sister and her husband, Bob, in the back. Three-and-a-half-year-old Jake tucked between aunt and uncle in his car seat, swinging boy legs in the space between the bucket seats. His soft-bodied Mickey Mouse strapped in with him, the one with tired ears from endless cuddling and dragging. Raffi's *Baby Beluga* cassette winded along with us.

It just didn't work out before, Sherry said, her voice thinning on *before*.

Before. When she visited from Denver when her brother was alive. Before. When her brother and I were a couple on the verge of being a family. Before. When I was six-months pregnant with Jake and that husband died on an icy mountain road. Before. When we all thought time was a given, not a luxury.

Wanna stop at the Quartz Creek Big Trees Trailhead on the way? Scot asked. It's just off the highway, he said. I hear the trees are enormous.

Eighty-degree September day. That shoulder month in the Pacific Northwest where it yo-yos between summer hot and fall cool. We peeled our sweaty selves out of our Volvo wagon with its cobalt-blue seats. We yanked at shorts and shirt hems. Sherry patted her short blonde hair, a mirror gesture her mom did too. I smoothed my long T-shirt over my mama belly. Pressed fingers to the mermaid girl I was growing, mermaid girl who fluttered, whose scales she'd shed in another five months.

Let's go! Jake shouted at preschooler speed. My soak-it-all-in boy. Full-of-wonder boy. The-world-is-mine boy.

In moments, gravel parking lot switched to dirt path. Our footsteps muffled by needles. In moments we were in the arms of giant Douglas firs. Bathed in forest. Earthy fungus smell. Cushy green moss and fog smell. A touch of something sweet. Forest incense where the sun baked the bark. We stood in a grove of giant firs so tall they shaded the sky. Mammoth old-growth trees stretched, stretched so all I could do was stare up, up, up. One stove pipe Douglas fir maybe 250 feet tall. So wide that even with all of us holding hands we couldn't circle it. We were hushed by beauty. By grandeur. By magic. Quiet. Calm. Fairy tale-like. This holy place washed over us. Seeped into our skin.

The five of us all grinned. All open mouths. I ached for words to pair with this beauty.

Holy shit! Jake said, neck arched, the crown of his head pressed to my hip, his hazel eyes to the canopy, to the specks of sun that filtered through these giants.

I had this beat of *Oh shit*. The aunt and uncle who saw us about every nine months since we lived in Seattle and they lived in Denver. I'd taught their sweet nephew to swear.

But Sherry and Bob didn't bristle. Nothing judgy from their mouths. They laughed. They belly-laughed.

Absolutely, Bob said, and grinned his full Uncle Bob grin that lit him from the inside out. Couldn't have said it better myself.

Standing in the grove of ancient Douglas firs with my family, this family tree shaped differently than I imagined it when I was early-pregnant with Jake. This family tree that included me, the family I was born to, the two families I married, the family I was forging. This tree with all its branches and roots, with all its space for home.

Jake leaned his perfect egg-shaped head into my belly. Pressed the him of him into his sister, his eyes straight at the sky.

Holy shit, he said again and my laugh bubbled bliss.

After

When I promised myself I'd never ski again, it was a keepable promise.

Then.

When Jake was eight and Maria four, we said Sure to spring break skiing. Other families we loved were going and maybe it was their excitement that moved me to Yes.

I was okay until I wasn't.

Driving to the mountain I squiggled in the passenger seat of our refrigerator-white Suburban. Feet up. Feet down. Me inked in a twitch. Breathed high and tight, air grazing the top lobes of my lungs. Lightheaded, I reminded myself I knew how to breathe, how belly breaths calmed my system, calmed my heart.

Mount Bachelor glistened in its snowsuit. Chair lifts stitched the slopes. Fir trees edged ski runs, branches heavy with fresh snow frosting. Sharp mountain air with its cold bite that pricked my lungs, that pricked memory. Me learning to ski at 10. Skiing in high school with my boyfriend and his family. Kent. Falling in love with Kent on cross-country skis, backcountry and downhill skis, the mountain under our boots and all around us.

I reminded myself that skiing, the skiing part, not the husband-dies-on-his-way-to-go part, was full of happy.

But the fear voice I'd carried for nine years was loud.

Once we were at the lodge, to side-eye fear, I amped up mama mode. Zipped and snapped kids in their one-piece ski suits, in helmets. Maria with her stick-straight honey-colored hair and her Cupid's bow lips, this daughter who looked like Scot. This bright sun day in a pink ski suit, in goggles that swallowed her little face.

I'm good, Jake said when I asked if he needed help with his helmet. Will you hold these? he asked and handed me his gloves. Him in a blue ski suit with frog-green trim. Helmeted and gloved and ready.

We grabbed skis and poles and thumped in our boots to their lesson. As panic snaked my spine, I had memories of Mom being afraid of water (lakes, ocean, pools) while she pretended she wasn't, peppering lakeshore time with fake cheer—Isn't this fun! —while she insisted we wore lifejackets when digging in the sand. Mom inherited water fear from her mom, whose sister drowned when they were girls. I always felt her terror even though she did her best to set it down.

I could choose. I unclenched, loosened my mama grip, turned to the sun and took a huge sun sip. Filled up with light and joy. Remembered my love for skiing. Turned that love to Jake and Maria, eager for them to discover their skiing joy, not be clamped by fear.

What a beautiful day to ski, I said, my arms out wide, taking in my kids, the sky, the mountain. You'll do great because you are great. Have the best time. We love you, I said with a full-throated grin, making a memory for all of us.

As Scot and I clomped back toward the lodge in our unbuckled ski boots, fear pummeled my insides.

Fear screamed, What were you thinking?

Fear double-screamed, This is the worst idea EVER.

I breathed deep and slow.

You okay? Scot asked, his brow furrowed behind the frames of his forest-green glasses.

Sure.

Liar.

Busted, I said, with one sharp Ha!

Then some tiny voice whispered, You're here. Start easy. Maybe you can.

I signed up for a beginner group lesson.

After we practiced falling over and standing back up for 20 minutes or so, the instructor told us he'd meet us at the bottom of the beginner bunny slope with its beginner rope tow.

Take your skis off and walk over if you need to, he said as he skated off in a comfortable glide, the back of his red instructor jacket leaning left then right.

I skated over. If you haven't skied, skating on skies is much like skating on skates. Weight shifting. Gliding. I've always enjoyed the ease of it. The push and glide like dancing. So I skated. Muscle memory. My body took over.

You've skied, the instructor said when I was the first student to reach him. Not a question.

I'm a beginner, I said, glad for the cover of dark-lensed goggles so maybe he couldn't see the lie.

Huh, was all he said.

I took two bunny runs with the bunny class. Followed instructions. Snowplowed in the wedge position—pizza slice the kids called it—front tips almost touching, tails wide apart.

You should be in a different class, the instructor said. I was so fear-blind I couldn't even remember his name.

I shook my head. I shook him off.

At the bottom of the third run, he told me he was moving me to another class.

This isn't your class, he said.

What if I want to stay?

Why?

Tears pooled at the foam edges of my goggles. Pulse throbbed in my ears. I watched the chairlift spin in its endless cycle behind him. Felt my fingertips cool in the standing still.

Too scared to ski more than the bunny slope even though I knew he was right. It wasn't my class.

Then. The scritch of a skier stopping close. The spray of snow on my purple rental skis.

How's it going? Scot asked and brushed snow off his beard. Grinned his Scot grin. He'd been skiing alone. Clocking runs while the rest of us clocked ski school.

How's the bunny hill? he asked and turned up his smile. He knew my plan. Pretend to be a beginner. Relearn. Start from the start.

My thunder heart slowed.

Wanna take a run? I asked Scot.

You pick the chair.

Thanks for helping me get started, I told the instructor. I think I remember how these things work.

Was I still shaky?

I was.

Was Scot his patient self?

He was.

In a few runs I parallel skied. No snowplow. No pizza wedge. Skis together, snaking down the slope by shifting my weight. Big toe to little toe. Little toe to big toe.

After lunch we took a joy run. The swish and turn, skiing at the edge of control/not-control all mashed together. And my body remembered. The happy of skiing. The freedom of zipping down a mountain, singing "I'm Free" by The Who.

For all the times I've said our memories are storied in our bodies, I forgot good memories are stored there too. The I-know-how-to-ski memories. The beauty of fast and slow down a mountain on a sunny spring day. Wind in my face. Body facing down the run. Knees bending to turn in down/up/down. The sound of skis cutting snow. As I carved paths, I remembered the intersection of fear and excitement: my growth plate.

That afternoon I chased my sweet Scot who always cuts the best trail.

I'd follow him anywhere.

Hearts in rocks. Clouds. Clover petals. Mussel shells splayed open. The spider web I spied one fall, heart shaped, spun by a rebel. The heart in melting snow I almost crunched while hiking a trail. Owl's face. Horse blaze. Elementary school valentines, sticky with glitter—with joy. The gliding foam heart on a skin-thin sheet of ocean, shapeshifting on wet sand. Floaty. Foamy. Loamy. Full of holes and light and hope. Weaver of dreams. Holder of bliss. Keeper of love.

After

The weight of the torch in my right hand, the striker in my left. My childhood wish to be a farrier woven in the *sss* of acetylene. I felt that sweet memory every time I turned the dial and heard gas hiss. I clicked the striker near the tip of the torch, made it spark, flame, then added oxygen. The whoosh of flame. Me in grin. My pilot light sparked too. I adjusted the gasses to reach the perfect, tiny blue cone of fire at the center of the wider flame. The flame I chased in metalsmithing class: my Thursday evening get-your-art-on class I played in for a few years when the kids were smallish.

Often when I lit the torch, I remembered ranch days when girl-me studied the farrier as he fit horseshoes to hooves, as he heated and pounded and shaped metal, as he clamped hooves between his chap-covered thighs and pounded shoes on with nails. A tickle in my chest, then and now, a joy blip. Fire is my happy place.

In class I learned ways of shaping metal: sawing, snipping, drilling, soldering, polishing, stamping, and more. I cut shapes, welded some together, broke some apart, started something new, didn't start something new. Scrap metal took on new meaning

235

for me as my tiny scrap pile bloomed. While I made a few rings and one fabulous round copper box with a silver lid and words stamped around the edges that we filled with air (Scot and kids and I breathed through straws, caught our breath inside my forged-from-fire box), I loved the process over product. How metal shape-changed with a little heat.

Making art on Thursday evenings brought me back to me. Sawing, filing, heating metal was mediation. Not at first. At first it was a punch to the nervous system, our teacher having us recite the steps of lighting the acetylene torch with its two tanks, gauges, tubing, and dials. She reminded us every Thursday we could *blow ourselves up* if we did it wrong.

One class time as I stared at the flame—at the white, yellow, blue of it—and heard again Don't stare too long! I flashed on a tree. A family tree. My family/my kids' family tree arted out of metal. I could fabricate leaves and twigs, build a metal tree or stitch leaves and branches to fabric or heavy paper. When I'd sketched our family tree before, copying the traditional pattern, I struggled with the trunk, the branches, with who goes where, and who twines with whom. Building it with fire, I could ditch the aged image and follow a shape.

I thought about the family tree I sketched in junior high where I wrote my mom and dads on heavy branches. One mom. Two dads: the one I was born to, and the one who came into my life at 10 and raised my sisters and me like we were his own.

You can't do that, my junior high teacher said when she squinted at my tree holding my mom and both her first and second husbands. Family trees are your direct lineage, my teacher went and likely tapped the toe of her practical pump against the speckled linoleum. Follow the instructions.

But I have two dads, I told her all those years ago, me folded into a desk with a hard seat, a hard writing surface.

Use the one who gave you his genes, she said, her pointer finger with its close-cut nail circling my sketch tumbling off the eight-by-eleven piece of paper.

Scot gave Jake everything but his genes. Our family tree? It has its own silhouette. Me as mom. Scot and Kent as dads. The Dad Kent side, sculpted more in the image of the tree of life, or maybe family trees found in the front of old bibles, since his parents were married 61 years, stayed married until their souls polished, until their bodies withered and died. No extra dads or added moms. No side branches. No secret children who found the family later. They stayed the mom-dad-daughter-son-no dog-family in the suburbs with wide streets and porch seats. The Dad Scot side was similar, even though Scot's dad died when Scot was 16 and his mom remarried. Her second husband wasn't a dad to Scot. He was for his mom.

Our little family quartet of Scot and me and Jake and Maria. We didn't draw hard lines. No who's on whose team. Kent's family stayed our family. Kids grew up knowing four sets of grandparents, knowing we are all family.

When Jake was nine and Maria five, the four of us around the kitchen table eating a Tuesday night dinner: pasta and bread with a chewy crust. Plus salad and a side of carrots since the kids only nibbled the edges of their salads, making carrots their fall-back veggie. Was it Jake's favorite pasta, carbonara? Or Maria's: no sauce, with butter and fresh parmesan only? That part of the memory is pickled.

I do know my mouth was full of salad.

He was my dad too, Maria said even though we hadn't been talking about Kent just then or any time that day or maybe even for days. She kicked her girl-legs under the gouged pine table. Sun haloed her sunbaked hair, more bumblebee than caramel, so it must have been summer. She scooped a forkful of pasta, eyes on her plate.

Jake snuck a bite of bread under the table to our dog, Eddie.

But he died, she said.

I about choked on my mouthful. I didn't.

Eyes on Scot. His eyes wide behind his glasses for a beat. Then a half smile, not a grimace. A half-lit smile. Because, yes, Kent was her dad too. We didn't differentiate family. All of us together in our family soup with two dads, even though one was dead. We'd done our job. Keeping the You Can Ask/Say Anything door open. Our kids knew it was safe. Speak your hearts; we'll hold them in tender hands.

I lit the torch and pictured forging our family tree. A family tree that was anything and everything. Same as I'd done with my actual family. I sculpted it in metal. I sculpted it in heart. I heated a copper leaf, watched it turn from reddish rust to gold, orange, pink. Welded it to a tiny branch. Scored Jake and Maria's names into leaves and fused them in the crown of the tree. I swallowed stickiness with its metal aftertaste from particles that floated and stuck.

After

Whatcha doing? Jake asked. Six feet tall. Slender hips. Swimmer build. Dark hair that waved right where mine did. Same cowlicks on our DNA. Molasses, gold-flecked eyes that leaned toward blue when he was lit up from the inside. Cleft chin and dimple like a thumb and fingerprint.

Me in yoga clothes, on my second cup of Saturday morning coffee, wondering if I needed a rain jacket for my morning hill walk.

Do you have time now? Jake asked.

For what, Bud?

For the box, he said, like I knew what he meant.

Box?

You know. He rolled his shoulders forward. Muscle shoulders from playing rugby and weight training.

The box, he said, bouncing his bare toes, all long and slender from a Kent branch of his family tree.

Kent's box.

The one I packed in 1987 when Jake was a mini. The one I filled with Kent objects. The one I labeled: "Do Not Open until 2003" in green sharpie.

O-oh, I said, a squiggle in my belly at the edges of my center.

Wet-clay skies. Steel wool clouds. Rain spit on the kitchen windows. Pounded the cherry blossoms. Ballet-pink blossoms with red veins would lace the sidewalk and grass in a dusting of pink after the skies calmed.

The box had shifted from bedroom closet to guest room closet to basement closet, from my 1970s tri-level to a 1970s split level to a three-story 1937 eclectic.

Every time I'd move the box past 2003, I'd ask: Wanna open this?

Nah, he said (15).

Not today, (17).

Not now, (20).

One box move, when I was cradling the box, Jake said: Ma, I don't want to upset you, but I didn't know him. Dad's my dad.

Pebbles-tossed-at-a-window feeling. Swollen-with-love feeling. Mush with gratitude for Scot as husband and dad, with Jake knowing: Dad's my dad.

All true.

And our story is more. Some days it feels best to be us, the Gudgers four. A foursome where the son looks like the mom and the daughter mirrors the dad. What the world sees. And yet. Our history is not a secret. Buried grief festers. I never wanted that. We keep Kent in the ride of our family through stories, through saying his name and remembering what he loved, noticing things he'd enjoy and saying so. Through keeping his family as our family.

Okay, I said that rainy Saturday. Of course. Let's open the box.

I'd learned through teen years that when there's an opening, take it: Can we talk? Yes. Now. Can I show you something? Yes. Now.

I'll make more coffee, he offered. Smiled at me.

I'll make it, I said. You get the box.

All those No thanks times, eclipsed by my now 22-year-old, who was ready to uncover what I'd packed when he was learning how to be a baby.

You want to open it? he asked, offering the cardboard box that smelled like dusty paper and memories.

It's yours, I said. I made it for you.

I followed him into the living room. Coffee cups in shaky hands. This moment I prepared for. This moment I couldn't prepare for.

Side by side. His long legs so much longer than mine. At six feet, people often wondered at him, at me, at 5'9" Scot, and asked where he got his height. From me, I'd say when I didn't want to say more. Because. He's clearly mine. The DNA that rivers through me rivers through him. Our Greek heritage ripples through us in our hair, eyes, and noses. I always joked I couldn't lose him at a county fair.

Wind drafted down the chimney, past the tiles, across the walnut-colored wood floors. Blips of cold seeped through the single-paned windows.

Can you tell me why today? I asked. My heart felt a little louder.

Just curious. There's a lot I don't know, he said, fingers thrumming my green sharpie words.

I have questions, he said.

I'm ready to start asking.

I pictured him. The man he was stepping into being. Pictured him with a backpack full of his own 10 essentials, with pages he'd written of his life so far and a blank journal to keep writing what he'd find next.

He sliced the packing tape. Peeled back the flaps.

Do you know what's in here? he asked. He lifted a T-shirt with "Dinosaur Days" on the left breast-pocket space. Lifted with the care of an anthropologist on a dig.

It's been so long since I packed it, I said, and felt a prick at my ponytail spot. True. And there was more.

I was so grief-full then, I told him, one hand on him, one hand on me. I honestly don't remember what I picked, what I hoped could tell Dad Kent stories.

You ready? Jake eyed me, then peered under the "Dinosaur Days" T-shirt.

After

J ake peeled back the flap of a large manila envelope and slid out papers: a copy of Kent's birth certificate, report cards, newspaper clippings of local science fairs he'd been in, his acceptance letter to Caltech where he went, and to MIT where he didn't. Jake stared at Kent's birth certificate with its tiny inked baby feet, like hospitals did in 1950.

So different from mine, he said, and turned the piece of paper over in his man-sized hands that mirrored Kent's hands.

True. When Scot adopted Jake, Jake's original birth certificate was sealed, following adoption laws.

Why? I asked our attorney and she half-shrugged. There's no room in the law for an adoption like yours, she said. Unless you want to make a new law, I suggest getting copies of his original birth certificate before the adoption is final and records are sealed.

When we registered Jake for Little League in Kindergarten because he wanted to play T-ball, Jake saw that his birth certificate looked different from the other kids'. His was simple. Name: Jacob Kent Gudger. Birthdate: April 15, 1987. It names me as Mother and Scot as Father, no ages, no cities. It names us all as Gudger. It says Jake was born in Tacoma, Washington. It has a fancy, official state seal. Not much else. It does kind of look like we typed it up.

I want to show you something, I said back home, post T-ball sign-up. I thumbed through the files and fished out his birth certificate from when he was born. The one with all the boxes filled in. The one that named Kent as Father and me as Mother. The one that said Kent was 37 because he had a birthday after he died and before Jake was born. The one that said he lived in Federal Way. The one that said I was 28 and lived in Federal Way too. The one with Jake's name as Neuberger. His weight: 6 pounds, 9 ounces. His length: 21 inches.

I placed the certificates next to each other: Jacob Kent Neuberger, Jacob Kent Gudger. Birthdate: April 15, 1987.

Jake leaned his five-year-old self into me. His head at the curve of my waist. My hand on his shoulder blade. Our bodies puzzled together.

He underlined Jacob Kent Neuberger with his pointer finger.

He underlined Jacob Kent Gudger.

These are both true, I said, and got body chills.

You are all of this, I said.

You are so much more.

How do you know someone you never met?

What's the essence of a human?

Can stories convey the extraordinariness of a person?

How do you love a parent who died before you were born?

How do they love you?

How do they parent you?

What's the legacy?

I wanted to give Jake all my Kent memories, plus memories that weren't mine. I wanted to give him memories Kent hadn't had time to live. Impossible, but there it was.

We sat there, thigh to thigh, on the down-filled couch that let you sink right in. I told him what I knew about Kent studying the stars. I told him how happy Kent was that Jake was coming. How we'd lay in bed at night. Me exhausted from growing our fish boy. Kent talking to Jake through my belly. Telling him math formulas. Playing Beethoven spliced with Stevie Ray Vaughn.

He was so ready to be a dad, I said, my heart wet with tears.

Why do you think he left?

We'd talked reincarnation plenty. I'd told Jake before how I had wondered endlessly in the early days why Kent was pulled back so young. I'd told him how eventually I stopped asking why and asked different questions: What if 36 years was the right number of years for Kent? What if he did everything he came to do? On that rain-splattered day, something else struck me.

I'll never know for sure, I started, but I have this belief that we make agreements before we enter a new life.

I sipped cooling coffee, chewed the edge of my bottom lip.

Kent committed to fathering you. I said those words and felt the squishy tears-coming feeling. I breathed past the soggy in my throat. But he didn't agree to stay. Me? I committed to being your mama, being Maria's mama. Being here for all of it.

My heart pinged in time to the rain. My heart pinged in the key of love.

I wish I'd known him, Jake said, his own tears wet his face. I wrapped him in my mama arms, wishing he was still little, wishing I could soothe his hurting heart.

Me too, I said while I held him close. I wish you'd known him too.

The rain rained. Just past the paned windows. The hard gush of spring spitting on glass.

Through pictures and diplomas and report cards. Through Kent's handwriting (It's just like mine! Jake said.) Through baseball mitt and polished geode (with its cloud-white center and lake-blue edges) and mini Norton motorcycle. Through straight-edged razor and slide rule and a T-shirt collection. In the end, it was Kent's black leather wallet with its bent corners. Shadows of a driver's license, credit cards, the picture he carried of me when I was in the second grade.

Can I carry it? Jake asked.

Of course. It's yours.

I'm going to carry it, he said. I just need to feel close to him.

After

I conjure Kent in dreamland.

Here you go, he says.

No prelude, no Hi, Beauty.

He hands me a box, sized like fruit boxes at the grocery store, bigger than the Kent box I'd boxed for Jake.

Dishes? I ask.

He wiggles his eyebrows like he used to.

I peel back the box flaps. Inside, light glows in threads, ropes, puddles of light. Rainbow-colored, white, a blue that turns up bright like sky and low like ocean. Orange and purple shades like the light orbs I saw in the catacombs in Paris when we walked with the dead, when we wandered with acres of bones.

I stare at my grinning dead husband, at his offering, all the light in a box. My heart pulses with the throbbing lights, this pull of me to them and them to me.

It's beautiful, I sigh. It feels like everything all wadded up, but how can that be? What, what is it?

Look, he says, like he said so often when he was a body walking the earth. All these lights? They're lifepaths. They're infinite possibilities, he says when I suck in my lips, make my I-still-don't-understand face.

Everything is light. Everything is energy. It's all the same. You've been here before and you'll be here again.

This buzz in my head, a pinging in the center of my forehead, in my third eye. The lights pulse in waves. Some with short wavelengths—more up, more down—some with long wavelengths, flatter looking. I think about the wave machine we played with in high school physics—waves we could see that helped us understand the waves we couldn't.

Why's this one the brightest? I ask, pointing to a thrumming rope of light, fat as a rope of licorice, the three-foot kind I loved as a girl and still do. This magnet of light, brighter than all the squiggly, straight, loopy lights.

Ha! Because it's you: it's the one you chose this time, he says. His electric-blue eyes turn up, more blue, more electric.

I dip my ear toward my shoulder. I don't understand.

Wormholes. All of time happening at once. Not happening at once. You choose.

Time's a construct, he adds. Always remember that.

Dizzy in my dream body. Listening with every cell of me. Be in wonder, my dream-self reminds me. Let go of what you think you know.

Go ahead and touch it, he says and stretches the box closer to me. It's full of cosmic goodness.

My heart drums in my ears as I lift the pulsing light rope, wind it around my index finger, stare at its glow. A wave of something zaps my body. Floods me with images: girl-me on horseback. Lisa and I dancing in pretend tutus. Drawing, writing, reading, fishing. Teen-me with my first love, fabricating life plans. College-me traveling Europe with a Eurail pass, sleeping on beaches in Greece, eating delicious, cheap street food. Out-of-college me straddling the Continental Divide, my body in X, my body like Winged Victory. Jan and I graduating U of W together, grinning in caps and gowns: her as undergrad, me with a masters. Kent shining his love light. Marriage. Flying in a float plane over glaciers in Alaska. Winding thorough the catacombs in Paris, that labyrinth of death, guided by light orbs. Widowed. Parents and sisters holding me when all my edges melted. Jake being born. Scot slipping into our lives. Maria being born. Kids growing. Soccer, rugby, skiing, snowboarding. Birthday parties. Kitchen table talks. Beaches, Disneyland, Europe, Africa (where I told Scot every day: If I'm dreaming, don't wake me. Where I kissed a giraffe). Maria marrying Stephen in the woods by our friends' home where we fabricated a wedding space out of benches and tulle and a giant metal-winged heart and fairy lights in Mason jars, and then the reception in our friends' art studio, everything lit with love. Jake marrying Karma Rose at a vineyard, then the reception at our farm. Me writing. Images as fast as a card shuffle where you think you're seeing individual cards. But are you?

Woah, I say, and Kent grins bigger, light pooling from his lips.

I stare back into the box, the bottom dropping deeper, bottomless. What had looked like a snarl of light shape-changes to spools of light, thick as climbing ropes, thin as spider thread.

Pick a different light, have a different life, he says. So simple.

I touch a light coiled like a ship's rope. I touch it and feel a daughter who looks like me with dark wavy hair and olive-tinted skin. As I imagine this daughter, different from Maria, the light drips through my fingers. I can't hold it.

Why's it fading?

Oh, he starts, chewing his upper lip and syphoning air through his teeth.

It's the one I chose. It's the one with you. The one where I live in your dreams now.

My heart cramps. That ancient ache through muscle and skin.

But the girl? I ask, as my throat shrinks to the size of a cocktail straw.

We would have had a daughter who looked like you. You know, if I'd stayed—

I don't—

It's okay. All these lights? Which path do you pick? Which door do you walk through? They all happened, are happening, will happen. No past. No future. Everything is now.

All at once?

You already know the answer, he says, and grins his perfect crooked-tooth grin.

After

I
t's a 911 call, I blurted when Liz's phone went to voicemail. Jake's wedding is tomorrow and I really need to talk to you. I'm a mess.

Then before I hung up I added: I love you.

We'd been prepping the farm for a month, cleaning and primping, getting ready for Jake and Karma Rose's wedding reception. We'd weeded and spread bark dust. Planted pots and flower boxes. Son-in-law Stephen had mowed and loved the huge spread of lawn into greenness. Son-in-law and nephew designed and built a dance floor, along with adding trim pieces to the house that I'd dreamed of since we bought the farmhouse and barn and arena and 23 acres.

The day before the wedding, Karma Rose grabbed my hand.

I want to show you something, she said, all glow, all bride beautiful. I made a family tree. I hope you like it.

And there on the willow tree that bordered the lawn, she'd strung pictures of little her, little Jake. Pictures of their siblings. Pictures of her mom getting married, her dad getting married. My favorite picture of Scot and I marrying with toddler Jake in Scot's arms, all decked out in his sailor suit and toddler grin. Plus Kent and I on our wedding day, with Kent's family, his sister, who would be here for the wedding. Wedding pictures of grandparents too.

Look, she said and pulled me around the tree with its bumpy bark while my heart was soaking in the images from all the wedding bliss days, all the love frozen for a hiccup with the click of a shutter.

And there on the front, was my favorite picture of Kent. A headshot a photographer girlfriend before me had taken. His face in three-quarters. Hand to his chin in his thinking pose. Chin resting on knuckles. Skyscraper-grey hair. Mouse-brown beard with streaks of nutmeg. Sky-blue eyes.

Do you like it? Karma Rose asked, her face lit with happy, her face lit with love.

It's beautiful, I said, and the tears I'd been swallowing swam their way up my throat, out the edges of my eyes.

I hope it's okay that we used this picture of Kent. We just want him to be here too.

Of course it is, I said. I blinked hard, staring off at the hayfield for a beat to catch my tears.

And look! she said, pointing to an oversized heart-shaped chalkboard at the foot of the tree. She'd written "Family Tree" in chalk, inside a heart that was bigger than any enormous box of Valentine's Day chocolates.

It's perfect, I told her, and hugged her a quick hug.

I'll be right back.

I scooted off, under the trellis with the rusted metal birds that waited in welcome, along the path we flanked with heart-shaped rocks—pocket-sized to hand-sized to steppingstone-sized. Rocks I had collected for years. Rocks that found me more than I found them. I sped up crossing the gravel driveway to the barn. Our red barn. Solace. Safe. Every time I stepped into the barn it was like stepping back to the best parts of my girlhood, where dreamer-me dreamed, where my imagination soared while I watched hay dust in the slivers of light that broke through the cracks. With each step away from the getting-readiness of the wedding, tears inked out and found their tracks on my cheeks. By the time I reached the barn I was full out bawling.

I called Liz.

My widow friend who was still my friend. While the other widows from my group from once upon a time had dropped off, I carried Liz in my heart pocket. We talked regularly and got together when we could.

When she didn't answer and I left that 911 message, I almost threw myself against a bale of hay. Like I used to when I was a girl.

What was wrong with me? I was happy and excited for Jake to get married. As happy for him as I'd been for Maria two years earlier when my joy bubbles were bigger than the sky. And. I felt a deep sorrow. A missing Kent sorrow that hadn't squeezed my heart in years.

Plunked on a hay bale, eyeing the chickens clucking around the yard—the one that liked to roost in the rhododendrons, the other that liked to follow me—I breathed in hay and dust and the sweet smell of horse manure. Familiar smells that called me home.

Just as I was thinking I could go back and help with wedding prep, my phone rang. Liz.

What's up? she said in her Liz way. I got your message and called as soon as I heard it.

Jake's getting married tomorrow, I said, launching right in. No warm-up.

And while I'm happy, I'm also so sad. Gawd I miss Kent. Deep and hard, like I haven't in so long.

My breath puddled on my upper lip.

Of course you miss him.

She didn't say, Aren't you happy for Jake? She didn't say, Just look at the positive side. She didn't say, But you have Scot. I loved her hard for not saying what others might, for knowing those things were also true and my heart was missing Kent.

He's missing one of the most important days of Jake's life, she said, and my tears that had slowed, amped up again.

He's supposed to be here, I said. And I know that sounds ridiculous since he's been dead over 31 years. Since I've built a beautiful life with Scot.

It doesn't, Liz said. It doesn't sound ridiculous.

Grief is grief. And remember, sometimes it's an asshole, she said, and we both laughed. And just like those early days, she added, and sucked in a big belly breath. We gotta feel it all.

Sky breath breezed through the barn, fluttered my hair, fluttered my heart.

I'm surprised at how hard it hit me today.

Here's the truth; I didn't want it to be hard. I didn't want this big-mouthed ache. I didn't want to miss the silent third parent as much as I was. I wanted Scot and me to be enough.

Huh, Liz said. I'm not surprised. What surprised me is that you didn't call earlier this week.

I yanked a piece of hay from a bale and worried it between my fingers.

I love you, she said. You're going to be okay. You're going to have a beautiful day tomorrow. You're going to witness your boy, your beautiful boy, get married and you're going to cry like a mama.

Her words. Her heart. They were a salve. And the heaviness I'd done my best to ignore lifted. It didn't disappear, but I could feel it soften, melt. My mushy heart, uncaged. And I knew I was enough. Scot and I were enough. I could hold those opposites like I'd always held opposites: missing Kent and being grateful for the family we'd loved into being.

Just then, Buckwheat, our goat that acted like a dog, trotted in the barn. He bleated his bleat that sounded so human. Buckwheat saying, It's okay, sister. You got this.

I patted him between his horns. He rubbed his rough, hairy belly against my thigh, eyed me with his cornflower-blue marble eyes, and I swear, he nodded at me then nodded outside. So I followed my furry friend. Back to sunshine. Back to our honey hayfield with the hay knee-high, perfect for pictures tomorrow as the sun would dip over the hill and the hay would turn golden, the sky turning fire.

Buckwheat agrees, I told Liz. Thank you for being an anchor all these years. I love you. Tomorrow I'll be here with my whole ocean heart. With grief and gratitude and all the beauty of this amazing life.

After

My boy cub turned man cub turned man still carries Kent's wallet. Kent's wallet now Jake's. He pulls it out at times to show me its worn corners and soft edges.

He showed me on his wedding day. This reminder. Holding things close that others held close. Objects that maybe carry a sprinkle of our dead beloved's stardust deep in creases.

He's in my hip pocket, Jake said, gliding his thumb on worn leather.

And here too, he said, tapping his breast pocket where he carried Kent's wedding ring, the one I gave Kent 35 years ago, the one I gave Jake the night before his wedding: a braid of yellow, white, and rose gold, size nine, a ring of gold. Just right to fill a crack in the kintsugi my boy inherited.

It's one way I get to have him here, Jake said and pulled his lips straight in for a beat.

I love you, Jake-O, I said, a swell of grace tears swelling, my heart thrumming. We all do.

Of course I thought of tiny-him, how I could circle his chest with my hands when he was a newborn, how he fit in the *O* of thumbs and middle fingers touching.

My boy, all man now in his dove-grey linen suit. In his galaxy-wide heart with his dimple smile. My phenomenal boy who came from stardust. Who stood on this day on the verge of husband with a partner who was fire to his water. His Karma. His Rose.

You ready, Bud? I asked, like he had asked me when Scot and I married when Jake was hip high.

Ready, Mama, he said and we both laughed.

As the music started. As we stepped out—Scot on one of Jake's arms, me on the other—a breath of wind on this windless day fluttered my skirt and played with Jake's hair. A wave of goosebumps splashed up my arms and I knew it was Kent. The silent third parent loving us on a gorgeous July day. This family forged from fire. This family forged from love.

Kent was there, we all said later. I felt him.

Did you? Jake asked. Karma Rose asked. Family and friends asked. Our honey-soaked hearts all said Yes. Yes, we did.

Jake and Karma Rose under the trellis her dad and his brother-in-law built. Adorned with flowers arranged by her grandma. This handmade, lovemade setting. Her granddad officiated, love plumping in all his words. Their tender vows. Choosing each other. Choosing each other again and again. As they stood in the evening sun, as they stood in their bliss glow, a hummingbird buzzed in, then out, flashing its emerald-green bowtie, this messenger of healing. This tiny bird that traveled between worlds and time and back again.

Then the reception at our farm. No swans or salty Puget Sound water. This time a sun-drenched hayfield with a Tuscan sun. Lights strung around the handmade dance floor. A tree full of family wedding pictures: grandparents, daughter-in-law's parents, me with my first husband, me with my now husband. Love lights shining. The air electric with magic.

At toast time Scot stood behind the bride and groom, cleared his throat, wiped a tear with his knuckle. He was all thanks.

Then.

And tonight I have a double toast, he started.

The well of tears that floated between my top ribs perked up.

Not all of you know, but Annie was married before I knew her.

I was elbows on the table. Hands to my mouth.

She was pregnant with Jake when her husband died tragically, he said.

Jake was two when Annie and I got married, he said.

When he made me a dad.

Blinked, blinked tears. Willed myself to breathe. Maria, next to me, her copper-blonde hair shining, slid her hand, a younger replica of mine, on my knee as anchor, then wrapped my hand with hers.

Then our family grew, he said.

And we had Maria.

I'm a lucky guy.

So my first toast is to Kent, he said and raised his glass. His upper lip quivered. His voice too.

To Kent Neuberger.

Who gave you life.

We wish you were here.

Shot through with love. A love infusion. Skies of love. Oceans of love. Galaxies. Love tsunami flooded my heart's fifth chamber, that intersecting chamber I grew through grief, I grew through love.

That day I knew, to the bone of me, to love hard. Love fierce. Pass love on.

Here's my heart.

Afterward

And Kent? I carry him in the bone of a dream.
I am more because of how I loved him.
I am more because of how I lost him.
I am more because grief is love.
I am washed in gratitude for marrying kindness, twice.

I am not who I was in my Before. I don't know who I'd be had Kent lived, had that lifepath played out. Before me. After me. Tendrilled together. All of me informing all of me. Grief transformed me. Grief's my superpower.

I am the intersection. I am joy formed around sorrow. I am See Beauty Everywhere. I am Always Love Bigger. I am There's Always Room for Another Love Story.

Acknowledgements

Of all the things I've done, writing is the weirdest, most humbling, best soul balm. Writing is where I meet myself. Where I find what I didn't know I lost. I write at my antique desk with all its nicks and gouges, jammed with family photos and tarot cards and heart rocks from all the beaches and beyond, and mini toy animals: elephants, a pig, a giraffe, a monkey riding a horse. Add Lord Ganesh, skulls, crystals, a seeded dandelion frozen in a square of Lucite, a piece of coal from when I walked a fire walk. Candles and incense, of course. My girlhood paint box that somehow, somehow made it through the gauntlet of pitching. Favorite quotes. A watercolor of our barn. Tiny glitter birds with magnets where feet should be, that my kids once placed around the house for me to find in delight when we were all much younger. Add a stack of falling over journals. Add love notes that ground me.

I write alone. Most all of the time. And the art of moving from words scratched, typed, plopped on a page, to re-arranging, finding shape, finding meaning, finding none—doesn't happen alone. Skies of gratitude to my village of writers and not-writers.

For the people I love and who love me back. Deep bow to all the cosmic goodness that had us dream this dream together. Without all of you this book wouldn't be.

Thank you Elizabeth Earley at Jaded Ibis Press for saying Yes to my words, for publishing beautiful books and seeing my memoir alongside the incredible work you bring to the world. To the kindest editor, Vanessa Daunais, an extraordinary reader and word mover. Thank you for hearing my voice and turning up its shine. Thank you, Carmen Peters, for your eyes and smarts, your sharp edits, your attention to detail. And Nicole Roberts for the gorgeous book cover design. You turned a dream vision into an actual book cover that made me swoon. I'm grateful to the entire Jaded Ibis Press team. My book is more because of all of you. My heart to yours: thank you.

Grateful bows to the editors of the following publications, in which these works in whole or part have appeared and are now stitched in my memoir: "The Lifejacket" (*The Rumpus*), "Fish Boy" (*Barren Magazine*), "A Murder of Crows" (*Winning Writers*), "Beating Heart" (*NAILED Magazine*), "Here's My Heart" (*Timberline Review*), and "Wings" (*Atticus Review*). Buckets of gratitude to all the other journals that have published my words, my voice. Deep bow.

All love to my good art friends who created the amazing heart art for my book. Thank you Karen Luke Fildes for the stunning cover. And Katie Guinn for the bisected and blooming hearts. You both added a layer of beauty that makes me swoon. Thank you for your massive talent, your forever curiosity, your beauty finding. And for the fabulous author picture: all my gratitude and love to Robin Damore, who has shot the best author pictures over the years and captured the most beautiful events of our lives: both of my kids' weddings.

All of me, all my heart atoms, thanks the beautiful humans who held me up, who shined a light, who said Yes You Can, while I wrote and revised and revised.

All heart thanks to my book doulas, who know my story and have loved me through it, who've helped me find the gold. You are the finest human beings, with extra helpings of hearts and smarts. I'm so lucky and grateful you're all in my life and I get to write with you: Christie Tate, Tanya Friedman, Lois Melina, and Carol Claassen. Flutter love to these amazing writers I'm lucky to share words with, lucky to call friends: Katie Guinn, Beth Cartino, Carol Fischbach, and Adam Swanson. I love you like water. Deep bow and huge love to the women I was blessed to share an early draft with, in the workshop Body of the Book through Corporeal Writing: Jewelie Randall, Kathleen Postma, Monica Welty, Mary Davies, Krista Dabakis Price, and Sue Moshofsky. Thank you for seeing what you saw then, for seeing more than I could.

All gratitude and love to the best writing partner in the universe; Mary Mandeville, who has been in all my writing circles, who has written and listened and been my truth meter from the start. These words wouldn't be these words without your care, your smarts, and heart. Thank you with all of me.

Kate Carroll de Gutes and Jen Violi. I love you like chocolate. Thank you for laughing and writing with me. For being quiet when I needed that too. Thank you for being my heart.

Thank you to the phenomenal mentors, the divine humans I've had the privilege of writing with, learning from, leaning into: Ann Hood, Cheryl Strayed, Janice Lee, Jen Pastiloff, and Melissa Febos.

All gratitude to Beth Bornstein Dunnington for creating writing circles where the alchemy of truth telling shines. Thank you, Beth, for your eyes and heart on my words. Thank you for answering the phone at weird hours. Thank you for your friendship, your kindness, and love.

Thank-you words feel puny for my gratitude to Lidia Yuknavitch, who passed me air for the deep dive, who showed me a side door to get out of my own way, who held the mic for me to amplify my voice. Thank you Lidia, phenomenal human, medicine woman, magic mermaid, bringer of light, for believing in me and all of us humans writing our stories. The writing world is a better place because of you and Corporeal Writing, with your group of creative geniuses who make magic. As Lidia says, her creativity is bigger than her. Thank the stars she doesn't keep it for herself.

To the beautiful humans beyond my family, who formed a human net in my deepest grief. Thank you for being the ones who showed up, rocked and walked and cuddled Jake, cooked food and encouraged me to eat it, turned a junk room into a baby room. All your mini and massive kindnesses are etched on my heart. Tom and Karen Alexander (I love you always), Debra De Haan (from USC and beyond, thank you for being an extraordinary friend), Aspasia and David Gortner (who folded me into their family, made room in their home and hearts for Jake and me, opened the door wider for Scot and even had us marry on their gorgeous deck), Leo and Trisha Lee (godparents to my kids, amazing friends who I barely knew in my Before and who leaned-in in my After), and Marilyn and Dick Layton (who held me up and introduced Scot and me). My beautiful widow squad: Charlene, Chris, Lisa, and Janelle. Thank you for holding in my stitching when I was un-stitched. Plus, bottomless thanks to the teaching staff at Bellevue Community College in my time there. Thank you for always being willing to step in, step up, teach a class, or tell my students they had the day off.

Thank you to my heart friends who love me up close, who hold the vision even when I am tired and need to set it down: Liz Marzano, Heidi Martincic, Rozanne Garmen, Sue Sullivan, Brenda Olson, Jane Kendall, Ron Gilbert, and Merrill Hendin. To say I couldn't have kept on without your love would be saying it too small. Thank you for laughing and crying with me, for sitting in the quiet, for naming me nicknames, for seeing beauty and silliness, for drinking coffee and more coffee with me.

My deepest gratitude and love to more friends who saw the best in me, who helped me remember who I am at my core: a woman with an oceanic heart. Thank you Dan Gibbons, Stacy Bellwood, Denny Damore, Chuck Bauschelt, and Courtney Hoch. You are ground and sky and I am so grateful our planets collided.

And always, always. Endless thanks to my families: the one I was born to, the families I married into, the family I grew.

All love and gratitude to my parents who gave me life, who loved me up close and from afar. Maria and J. Upton who taught me to look for beauty and see the good. David and Claudia Pease who taught me to look forward, not back. Thank you to my two beautiful sisters, Jan Pease and Lisa Pease, who I'm lucky to go around with this lifetime, past lifetimes, and likely next ones too. You make sistering easy and I am oh so completely grateful for your hearts. Plus, family love to all the dogs I loved along the way. Especially Eddie the Wonder Dog, curled up in my office, guiding the early drafts.

Skies of love and gratitude to Scot's family. His parents, Adele Gudger Smith, Jack Gudger, and Lennard Smith; his beautiful sisters Nancy Raiha and Sue Biggs, plus their fabulous husbands/ best brother-in-laws Glenn Raiha and Jack Will; our nephews and niece who shine their creative selves in the world. You've all made this married life so much sweeter and deeper.

Huge love to Kent. Who showed me a love profound like no one before him. Who taught me to stretch my heart. Who left too soon. I'll never say I'm grateful you died too young. I'll always say I'm grateful you gave me our son. I'll always say I'm grateful for the ways I learned a deeper, wider love, more compassion, a boundless acceptance of grief in all its forms. I love you through the stars, beyond the Rosette Nebula.

Buckets of love to Kent's family. His parents Gwen and Frank Neuberger, and his brother-in-law Bob Howerton, who glide and cartwheel with him past the Milky Way. His sister Sherry Howerton, who will always be my sister too, and her beautiful daughters and their amazing families. Thank you for being nieces and great-nieces and great-nephew. Families are who we choose and I choose you all, over and over. I love being part of this family. Thank you for wrapping your hearts with mine.

I celebrate who is here and who isn't. And we're all here. To all my dead ancestors who opened space for my book to find its way into the world: I'm mush with gratitude.

Endless love to more beloveds who swim in the night sky: Stepdad J., Dad, Mom-in-law Adele Smith, grandparents Sally and Mike, Elsie and David, Lil and Evon, plus dear friends Velinda Kelly and Carl Madson who also left too soon. My heart is comforted thinking of you all dipping in and out of the stars together, slip-sliding through the Milky Way. Thank you for loving me through the veil.

To my beloved children, Jacob Zavita and Maria Gibson, and their beloved spouses, Karma Rose Zavita and Stephen Gibson. Thank you for making me a mom and mom-in-law. You are brilliant love planets in my solar system. Thank you for making family with me, for being in the dance, for shining love. It is pure joy to see you building your lives, loving your people, being generous and kind. I carry you all in my heart's fifth chamber.

Most of all, all my love to my sweet husband, my north star, my Scot. You are the bass beat, the glue, the heart, and I couldn't love you more (although I will tomorrow). Thank you for always making room at the table for all of me, all of us. For understanding and welcoming Kent in all of our lives. Thank you for choosing me, over and over, for joying up my days and nights. You are a dream beyond a dream, and I'm so grateful I get to dance this holy, full-of-wonder-and-delight life with you. Here's my heart. It's yours.

Printed in the USA
CPSIA information can be obtained
at www.ICGtesting.com
JSHW010314280823
47207JS00002B/10